Notes Of
A Twenty-Five Years' Service
In The Hudson's Bay Territory
Vol. I

by
John Mclean

Notes Of
A Twenty-Five Years' Service
In The Hudson's Bay Territory
Vol. I
by John Mclean

Copyright © 2024

All Rights reserved.

No part of this publication may be reproduced, stored in a retrieval system, or transmitted in any form or by any means, electronic, mechanical, photocopying or Otherwise, without the written permission of the publisher.
The author/editor asserts the moral right to be identified as the author/editor of this work.

ISBN: 978-93-64287-77-7

Published by

DOUBLE 9 BOOKS
2/13-B, Ansari Road
Daryaganj, New Delhi – 110002
info@double9books.com
www.double9books.com
Tel. 011-40042856

This book is under public domain

ABOUT THE AUTHOR

John McLean was a notable figure in the history of Canada, particularly known for his extensive service with the Hudson's Bay Company during the 19th century. He played a significant role in the exploration, trade, and settlement of the Hudson's Bay Territory, leaving behind a detailed memoir that provides valuable historical insight. McLean's career with the Hudson's Bay Company spanned twenty-five years, during which he worked in various capacities, including as a trader and explorer. His experiences brought him into frequent contact with Indigenous peoples of the region, and his memoir reflects his interactions and observations of their cultures, traditions, and way of life. Born in Scotland, McLean ventured to North America to pursue opportunities with the Hudson's Bay Company, driven by the allure of adventure and the prospects of economic gain through the fur trade. His writings not only document his personal experiences but also offer a window into the broader historical context of European exploration and colonial expansion in western Canada. McLean's contributions to the understanding of early Canadian history are significant, as his firsthand accounts provide valuable details about the challenges, successes, and complexities of life in the Hudson's Bay Territory during the 19th century. His memoir continues to be studied by historians and researchers interested in the fur trade era and the interactions between Indigenous peoples and European settlers in North America.

CONTENTS

PREFACE 7
CHAPTER I 9
CHAPTER II 12
CHAPTER III 15
CHAPTER IV 21
CHAPTER V 26
CHAPTER VI 30
CHAPTER VII 34
CHAPTER VIII 40
CHAPTER IX 45
CHAPTER X 49
CHAPTER XI 56
CHAPTER XII 60
CHAPTER XIII 66
CHAPTER XIV 72
CHAPTER XV 80
CHAPTER XVI 88
CHAPTER XVII 94
CHAPTER XVIII 97
CHAPTER XIX 103
CHAPTER XX 110
CHAPTER XXI 114

PREFACE

The writer's main object in first committing to writing the following Notes was to while away the many lonely and wearisome hours which are the lot of the Indian trader;—a wish to gratify his friends by the narrative of his adventures had also some share in inducing him to take up the pen.

While he might justly plead the hacknied excuse of being urged by not a few of those friends to publish these Notes, in extenuation of the folly or presumption, or whatever else it may be termed, of obtruding them on the world, in these days of "making many books;" he feels that he can rest his vindication on higher grounds. Although several works of some merit have appeared in connexion with the subject, the Hudson's Bay territory is yet, comparatively speaking, but little known; no faithful representation has yet been given of the situation of the Company's servants—the Indian traders; the degradation and misery of the many Indian tribes, or rather remnants of tribes, scattered throughout this vast territory, is in a great measure unknown; erroneous statements have gone abroad in regard to the Company's treatment of these Indians; as also in regard to the government, policy, and management of the Company's affairs;—on these points, he conceives that his plain, unvarnished tale may throw some new light.

Some of the details may seem trivial, and some of the incidents to be without much interest to the general reader; still as it was one chief design of the writer to draw a faithful picture of the Indian trader's life,—its toils, annoyances, privations, and perils, when on actual service, or on a trading or exploring expedition; its loneliness, cheerlessness, and ennui, when not on actual service; together with the shifts to which he is reduced in order to combat that ennui;—such incidents, trifling though they may appear to be, he conceives may yet convey to the reader a livelier idea of life in the Hudson's Bay Company's territories than a more ambitious or laboured description could have done. No one, indeed, who has passed his life amid the busy haunts of men, can form any just idea of the interest attached by the lonely trader to the most trifling events, such as the arrival of a stranger Indian,—the coming of a new clerk,—a scuffle among the Indians,—or a sudden change of weather. No one, unaccustomed to their "short commons," can conceive the intense, it may be said fearful, interest and excitement with which the issue of a fishing or hunting expedition is anticipated.

Should his work contribute, in any degree, to awaken the sympathy of the Christian world in behalf of the wretched and degraded Aborigines of this vast territory; should it tend in any way to expose, or to reform the abuses in the management of the Hudson's Bay Company, or to render its monopoly less injurious to the natives than hitherto it has been; the writer's labour will have been amply compensated. Interested as he still is in that Company, with a considerable stake depending on its returns, it can scarcely be supposed that he has any intention, wantonly or unnecessarily, to injure its interests.

    Guelph, Canada West,
    1st *March*, 1849.

CHAPTER I

That part of British North America known by the name of the Hudson's Bay territory extends from the eastern coast in about 60° W. long. to the Russian boundary in 142° W.; and from the Gulf of St. Lawrence, along the Ottawa River and the northern shores of Lakes Huron and Superior, and thence to the boundary line of the United States; extending in latitude thence to the northern limit of America; being in length about 2,600 miles, and in breadth about 1,400 miles. This extensive space may be divided into three portions, each differing most materially in aspect and surface. The first and most extensive is that which is on the east, from the Labrador coast, round Hudson's Bay, northward to the Arctic region, and westward to the Rocky Mountains. This is entirely a wooded district, affording that plentiful supply of timber which forms so large a branch of the Canadian export trade. These interminable forests are principally composed of pines of large size, but which towards the northern boundary are of a very stinted growth. Another portion is the prairie country, reaching from Canada westward to the Rocky Mountains, and intersected by the boundary line of the United States. In general, the soil is rich alluvial, which being covered with luxuriant herbage, affords pasturage for the vast herds of wild buffaloes which roam over these extensive plains. The western part is that which lies between the Rocky Mountains and the Pacific Ocean, including the Oregon territory, which was likely to have led to a serious misunderstanding between Great Britain and the United States.

These extensive portions are divided by the Hudson's Bay Company into four departments, and these departments are again subdivided into districts. At the head of each department and district a chief factor or chief trader generally presides, to whom all the officers within their respective jurisdictions are amenable. Those in charge of posts, whatever may be their rank, are subject to the authority of the person at the head of the district; and that person receives his instructions from the superintendent of the department. The whole affairs of the country at large are regulated by the Governor and Council, and their decisions again are referred, for final adjustment, to the Governor and Committee in London.

The Montreal department comprehends all the districts and posts along the Gulf and River St. Lawrence; also the different posts along the banks of the Ottawa and the interior country. The depôt of the department is at Lachine, where all the returns are collected, and the outfits prepared.

The southern department has its depôt at Moose Factory, in James's Bay; it includes the districts of Albany, Rupert's House, Temiscamingue, Lake Huron, and Lake Superior, together with several isolated posts along the shores of the Bay.

The northern department is very extensive, having for its southern boundary the line which divides the British from the American territories, sweeping east and west from Lac La Pluie, in 95° W. long, and 49° N. lat. to the Rocky Mountains in 115° W. long.; then, with the Rocky Mountains for its western boundary, it extends northward to the Arctic Sea. The whole of this vast country is divided into the following districts: Norway House, Rainy Lake, Red River, Saskatchewan, English River, Athabasca, and McKenzie's River. The depôt of this department is York Factory, in Hudson's Bay, and is considered the grand emporium; here the grand Council is held, which is formed of the Governor and such chief factors and chief traders as may be present. The duty of the latter is to sit and listen to whatever measures the Governor may have determined on, and give their assent thereto, no debating or vetoing being ever thought of; the Governor being absolute, his measures therefore more require obedience than assent. Chief traders are also permitted to sit in council as auditors, but have not the privilege of being considered members.

The Columbia department is bounded on the east by the Rocky Mountains, and on the west by the Pacific Ocean. An ideal line divides it on the south from the province of California, in lat. 41° 30'; and it joins the Russian boundary in lat. 55°. This, although a very extensive department, does not consist of many districts; New Caledonia is the principal, situated among the Rocky Mountains, and having several of its posts established along the banks of the Fraser River, which disembogues itself into the Gulf of Georgia in nearly 49° lat. and 122° W. long. The next is Colville, on the Columbia River, along with some isolated posts near the confluence of the same river. The *forts*, or trading posts, along the north-west coast, have each their respective commander. The shipping business is conducted by a person appointed for that purpose, who is styled, *par excellence*, the head of the "Naval department." The Company have a steamboat and several sailing vessels, for the purpose chiefly of trading with the natives along the coast. The primary object, however, is not so much the trade, as to keep brother Jonathan in check, (whose propensity for encroaching has of late been "pretty much" exhibited,) and to deter him from forming any establishments on the coasts; there being a just apprehension that if once a footing were obtained on the coast, an equal eagerness might be manifested for extending their locations into the interior. Strong parties of hunters are also constantly employed along the southern frontier for the purpose of destroying the fur-bearing animals in that quarter; the end in view being to secure the interior from the encroachments of foreign interlopers. The depôt of this department is at Fort Vancouver, on the Columbia River.

The Hudson's Bay Company, as it at present exists, was incorporated in the winter of 1820-21, a coalition having been then formed with the North-West Company. Upon this taking place, an Act of Parliament was obtained which gave them not only the possession of the territory they had originally held by virtue of their royal charter, but also investing them with the same rights and privileges conferred by that charter in and over all the territories that had been settled by the North-West Company for a term of twenty-one years.

The Governor, Deputy-Governor, and managing Committee, are, properly speaking, the only capitalists. The stock is divided into one hundred shares; sixty of which their Honours retain for themselves; and the remaining forty are divided among the chief traders and chief factors, who manage the affairs in the Indian country. A chief factor holds two of these shares, and a chief trader one; of which they retain the full interest for one year after they retire, and half interest for the six following years. These cannot be said to be stock-holders, for they are not admitted to any share in the executive management; but according to the present system they are termed Commissioned Officers, and receive merely the proceeds of the share allotted to them. They enjoy, however, one very superior advantage,—they are not subjected to bear their share in any losses which the Company may sustain. It is generally reckoned that the value of one share is on an average about 350*l.* sterling a-year. By the resignation of two chief traders, one share is at the Company's disposal the year after, which is then bestowed on a clerk. When two chief factors retire, a chief trader is promoted in like manner. Promotion also take place when the shares of the retired partners fall in.

CHAPTER II

I entered the service of the Company in the winter of 1820-21, and after passing my contract at Montreal in the month of January, I took up my residence for the remainder of the season with a French priest, in the parish of Petit le Maska, for the purpose of studying the French language. The Padre was a most affable, liberal-minded man, a warm friend of England and Englishmen, and a staunch adherent to their government, which he considered as the most perfect under the sun. The fact is, that the old gentleman, along with many others of his countrymen who had escaped from the horrors of the French Revolution, had found an asylum in our land of freedom, which they could find nowhere else; and the personal advantages that had accrued to him from that circumstance, naturally induced a favourable disposition towards his benefactors, their laws, and their institutions. Though the Padre was extremely liberal in his political opinions, his management of his worldly affairs bore the stamp of the most sordid parsimony. He worshipped the golden calf, and his adoration of the image was manifest in everything around him. He wore a cassock of cloth which had in former times been of a black colour, but was now of a dusky grey, the woollen material being so completely incorporated with dust as to give it that colour. His table was furnished with such fare as his farm produced, with the addition, on particular occasions, of a bottle of *black strap*. A charming nymph, of some fifty years of age or so, had the management of the household, and discharged all her duties with strict decorum and care. I have the beauties of her person in my mind's eye to this day. She was hump-backed, short-necked, and one-eyed, and squinted bewitchingly with the remaining one: she had a short leg and a long one, a high shoulder and a low. In short, the dear creature seemed to be formed, or rather deformed, by the hand of nature on purpose to fill the situation of housekeeper for a priest,—so that whatever might be his age, no scandal could possibly attach itself to him from such a housekeeper. The man-servant was directly the counterpart of the charming Marguerite; he also was far advanced in the vale of years, and was of a most irascible temper. To stir up Joseph to the *grinning point* was a very easy matter; and his frantic gesticulations, when thus goaded to wrath by our teasing pleasantries, (there were two other young gentlemen beside myself,) were of the most extraordinary description, and afforded infinite amusement. We never failed to amuse ourselves at

Joseph's expense, when the Padre's absence permitted our doing so with impunity,—especially as a small present of tobacco, which was always kept at hand for such occasions, soon made us friends again. But it sometimes happened that such jokes were carried too far, so as to render the offering of *incense* quite unacceptable, when the touch of *metal* could alone produce the desired effect.

I remained with Father Gibert until spring, and shall take leave of him by relating an anecdote or two illustrative of his loyalty and benevolence. Some time during Madison's unprovoked war with Great Britain, an alarm came from the upper part of the parish of which Father Gibert was *curé*, that a party of Americans had been seen marching down the country. The *Capitaine* of militia, who was the *curé's* next door neighbour, was immediately sent for, and by their joint influence and authority a considerable number of *habitans* were soon assembled under arms, such as they were. The Father then shouldering his musket, and placing himself at the head of his parishioners, led them into his garden, which was enclosed by a picket fence, and bordered on the highway. Here the loyal band took their stand under cover of the fence, waiting to give Jonathan a warm reception the moment he came within reach. The supposed Americans proved to be a small detachment of British troops, and thus the affair ended.

On another occasion during the same period the Padre's loyalty and good humour were manifested, though in a different manner. While amusing himself in the garden one day, he overheard two Irish soldiers engaged in conversation to this effect:—

"You know that the ould boy asks every body afore he gives any praties, if they belong to St. Patrick; well, is it a hard matter to tell him we do, agrah?"

"Sure you'd be telling a lie, Paddy!"

"Never mind that," said Paddy, "I'll spake."

The old gentleman immediately returned to the house, and entering by a back door, was snugly seated in his arm-chair, book in hand, when the two Hibernians were admitted.

"Well, my boys, what is your business with me?"

"We would be wanting a few praties, if your Riverence could spare them."

"Aha! you are from Ireland, I perceive. Irishmen very fond of potatoes! Well, my boys, I have a few remaining, and you shall have some if you belong to St. Patrick."

"Faith, and it is all as your honour says; we are Irishmen, and we belong to St. Patrick."

The old gentleman ordered Joseph to supply them with the "blessed root," without any further parley. Then addressing the speaker in a voice of assumed choler, exclaimed:—

"You are a great raskail! does your religion teach you to tell lies ? You are Protestant both of you. However, if you do not belong to St. Patrick, you belong to the King of England, and I give my potatoes for his sake. But you must never try to impose upon an old priest again, or you may not come so well off."

CHAPTER III

I arrived at Montreal about the beginning of May, and soon learnt that I was appointed to the post at Lake of Two Mountains. The Montreal department was headed at that time by Mr. Thane, a man of rather eccentric character, but possessed of a heart that glowed with the best feelings of humanity. I was allowed to amuse myself a few days in town, having directions however to call at the office every day, in case my services should be required. The period of departure at length arrived. I was one evening accosted by Mr. Thane in these terms:—"I say, youngster, you have been trifling away your time long enough here; you must hold yourself ready to embark for your destination to-morrow morning at five o'clock precisely. If you delay one moment, you shall have cause to remember it." Such positive injunctions were not disregarded by me. I was of course ready at the time appointed, and after all the hurry, had the honour of breakfasting with my commander before departing; but the woful and disheartening accounts of the hardships and privations I was to suffer in the country to which I was to proceed, fairly spoiled my appetite. I was told that my only lodging was to be a tent, my only food Indian corn, *when I could get it*; and many other *comforts* were enumerated with the view of producing a certain effect, which my countenance no doubt betrayed, whilst he chuckled with the greatest delight at the success of his jokes. I took leave, and found myself that evening at the Lake of Two Mountains. On my arrival, a large building was pointed out to me as the Company's establishment, to which I soon found admittance, and was, to my great surprise, ushered into a large well furnished apartment. Tea had just been served, with a variety of substantial accompaniments, to which I felt heartily disposed to do ample justice, after my day's abstinence. This was very different entertainment from what I had been led to expect in the morning; would it had been my lot to be always so agreeably deceived!

The village of the Lake of Two Mountains is inhabited by two distinct tribes of the aborigines—viz. the Iroquois and the Algonquins; the latter are a tribe of the Sauteux nation, or Ojibbeway, and live principally by the chase. The former cultivate the soil, and engage as voyageurs, or in any other capacity that may yield them the means of subsistence. They are a very hardy industrious race; but neither the habits of civilized life, nor the influence of the Christian religion, appear to have mitigated, in any material degree, the ferocity that characterized their pagan ancestors. Although they do not pay great deference to the laws of God, they are sufficiently aware of the consequences of violating the laws of man, and comport themselves accordingly.

The Catholic seminary and church, along with the gardens of the establishment, almost divide the village into two equal parts; yet this close proximity does not appear to encourage any friendly intercourse between the two tribes. They in fact seldom pass their respective limits, and, with few exceptions, cannot converse together, the language of the one being unintelligible to the other.

The Company established a post here in the spring of 1819, and when I arrived it was in charge of Mr. Fisher, then a senior clerk. He had two other clerks under him, besides myself, a like number of *attachés*, two interpreters, two servants, and a horse to ride upon. With such an establishment to rule over, need it be matter of surprise that our *bourgeois* was in his own estimation a magnate of the first order? *N'importe,*—whatever might be his vanity, he possessed those qualities which constitute a first-rate Indian trader, and he required them to fill successfully his present situation. A number of petty traders were settled in the village, who, whenever the Company entered the lists against them, laid aside the feuds that subsisted among themselves, and joined to oppose their united efforts against the powerful rival that threatened to overwhelm them all. The spring fur campaign was about to open when I made my *début* at the post. The natives being daily expected from the interior, all parties watched their arrival night and day. This was not a very harassing duty to us, as we relieved each other; but the situation of our superior was exceedingly irksome and annoying. The moment an Indian canoe appeared (the Indians always arrived at night), we were ordered to apprize him of it; having done so, he was immediately at the landing-place, our opponents being also there, attending to their own interests. Some of the natives were supplied by the Company, others by the petty traders; and according as it happened to be the customers of either that arrived, the servants assisted in unloading the canoes, conveying the baggage to their houses, and kindling a fire. Provisions were furnished in abundance by both parties. While these preliminary operations were being performed by the servants, the traders surrounded the principal object of their solicitude — the hunter; first one, then another, taking him aside to persuade him of the superior claims each had on his love and gratitude. After being pestered in this manner for some time, he, (the hunter,) eventually allowed himself to be led away to the residence of one of the parties, where he was treated to the best their establishment afforded; the natives, however, retaining their furs, and visiting from house to house, until satiated with the good cheer the traders had to give them, when they at length gave them up, but not always to the party to whom they were most indebted. They are generally great rogues; the sound of the dollars, which the Company possessed in abundance, often brought the furs that were due to the petty trader to the Company's stores; while some of our customers were induced by the same argument to carry their furs to our rivals.

For a period of six weeks or so, the natives continued to arrive; sometimes in brigades, sometimes in single canoes; during the whole of this period we were occupied in the manner now described, day and night. So great was the pressure of business, that we had scarcely time to partake of the necessary refreshment. When they had at length all arrived, we enjoyed our night's rest, if indeed our continually disturbed slumbers could be called rest:—what with the howling of two or three hundred dogs, the tinkling of bells with which the horses the Indians rode were ornamented, the bawling of the squaws when beaten by their drunken husbands, and the yelling of the savages themselves when in that beastly state, sleep was impossible,— the infernal sounds that continually rent the air, produced such a *symphony* as could be heard nowhere else out of Pandemonium. No liquors were sold to the natives at the village, but they procured as much as they required from the opposite side of the lake. Some wretches of Canadians were always ready, for a trifling consideration, to purchase it for them; thus the law prohibiting the sale of liquor to the Indians was evaded. After wallowing in intemperance for some time, they ultimately submitted to the authority of the priests, confessed their sins, received absolution, and became *good Christians* for the remainder of the season. If any indulged in the favourite vice—a few always did—they were confined to their quarters by their families. After attending mass on Sundays, they amused themselves playing at ball, or running foot races; and it was only on such occasions they were seen to associate with their neighbours the Iroquois. They took opposite sides in the games; small stakes were allowed, merely to create an interest in the issue of the contest. The chiefs of both tribes sat smoking their pipes together, viewing the sports in silent gravity, and acting as umpires in all cases of doubt between the parties. They, in fact, led a glorious life during the three months they remained at the village; that period was to them a continued carnival. The best fare the country afforded—the best attire that money could procure—all that sensuality, all that vanity could desire—their means permitted them to enjoy. Their lands not having been hunted on during the war, the beaver multiplied at an extraordinary rate, and now swarmed in every direction. Every individual belonging to the tribe might then have acquired an independent fortune. They arrived at the village, their canoes laden with furs; but the characteristic improvidence of their race blinded them to future consequences. Such was their wasteful extravagance, that the money obtained by the sale of their furs was dissipated ere half the summer season was over. The traders supplied them afterwards with all requisites at a *moderate* per centage; and when they embarked in autumn for their hunting grounds, they found themselves deeply involved in debt, a few only excepted.

In the course of this summer, some of our opponents foreseeing the probable issue of the contest they were engaged in, proposed terms of capitulation, which were in most instances readily assented to by the Company; the inventories and outstanding debts were assumed at a certain valuation. They retired from the field, some with annuities for a stipulated period, while to others a round sum of money was granted; in either case the party bound himself, under certain penalties, not to interfere in the trade for a stated period of time.

In this manner the Company got rid of all petty opponents, with the exception of two who continued the unequal contest. By the latter end of August the natives had all started for the interior, leaving behind only a few decrepit old men and women. The scene was now completely changed; a death-like stillness prevailed where but a few days before all was activity, bustle and animation. Two of my brother scribes were ordered to the interior; one[1] to the distant Lake Nipissingue, the other to the Chats. Mr. Fisher set off to enjoy himself in Montreal, Mr. Francher, the accountant, being appointed *locum-tenens* during his absence. Another young Scot and myself, together with two or three non-descripts, formed the winter establishment. Having just quitted the scenes of civilized life, I found my present solitude sufficiently irksome; the natural buoyancy of youthful spirits, however, with the amusements we got up amongst us, conspired to banish all gloomy thoughts from my mind in a very short time. We—my friend Mac and myself—soon became very intimate with two or three French families who resided in the village, who were, though in an humble station, kind and courteous, and who, moreover, danced, fiddled and played whist.

There was another family of a different status from the others, that of Capt. Ducharme, the king's interpreter, a kind-hearted, hospitable man, who frequently invited us to his house, where we enjoyed the charms of polished society and good cheer. The captain's residence was in the Iroquois division of the village; this circumstance led us to form another acquaintance that for some time afforded us some amusement, *en passant*. We discovered that a very ugly old widow, who resided in that quarter, had two very pretty young daughters, to whom we discoursed in Gaelic; they answered in Iroquois; and in a short time the best *understanding* imaginable was established between us, (Mac and myself, be it always understood.) No harm came of it, though; I vow there did not; the priests, it seems, thought otherwise. Our acquaintance with the girls having come to their knowledge, we were one day honoured with a visit from the Iroquois padre; the severe gravity of whose countenance convinced us at a glance of the nature of his mission. I must do him the justice to say, however, that his address to us was mild and admonitory, rather than severe or reproachful. I resolved from that moment to speak no more Gaelic to the Iroquois maidens; Mac continued his visits.

We always amused ourselves in the evenings with our French *confrères*, (whom I have mentioned as "nondescripts," from the circumstance of their being under no regular engagement with the Company,) playing cards or fiddling and dancing. We were on one occasion engaged in the latter amusement *en pleine midi*—our *Deputy* Bourgeois being one of the party, and all of us in the highest possible glee, when lo! in the midst of our hilarity, the hall door flew open and the *great man* stood sternly before us. The hand-writing on the wall could scarcely have produced a more startling effect on the convivial party of old, than did this unexpected apparition upon us. We listened to the reprimand which followed in all due humility, none more crest-fallen than our worthy Deputy. Mr. Fisher then opened his portmanteau and drew forth a letter, which he presented to my friend Mac, exclaiming in a voice of thunder, "Read that, gentlemen, and hear what Mr. Thane thinks of your conduct." We read and trembled; Mac's defiance of the authority of the priests offended them mortally; a formal complaint was consequently preferred against the innocent and the guilty, (although there was no guilt in fact, unless *speaking Gaelic* to the wood-nymphs could be so construed,) and drew upon us the censures this dreadful missive conveyed. The magnate remained a few days, and on his departure for town, we resumed our usual pastimes, but selected a different *path* to Captain Ducharme's. The Fathers had requested, when this establishment was first formed, that some of the Company's officers should attend church on Sundays for the purpose of showing a good example to the natives. I did so, on my part, very regularly until Christmas Eve, when having witnessed the ceremonies of the midnight mass, I determined on remaining at home in future. I shuddered with horror at the idolatrous rites, as they appeared to me, which were enacted on that occasion. The ceremonies commenced with the celebration of mass; then followed the introduction of the "Infant Jesus," borne by four of the choristers, attired in surplices of white linen. The image being placed by them on a sofa in front of the altar, the superior of the seminary made his debut, retiring to the railing that surrounds the altar, when he knelt, and bending low his head apparently in devout adoration, he arose, then advanced two steps towards the altar and knelt again; he knelt the third time close to the side of the image, which he devoutly embraced, then withdrew: the younger priests performed the same ceremonies; and after them every one of their congregation: yet these people protest that their religion has no connexion with idolatry, and that the representations of Protestants regarding it are false and calumnious. If we credit them, however, we must belie the evidence of our own senses; but the fact is, there are not a few Roman Catholics who speak with very little *respect* themselves of some of these mummeries.

> **Footnote 1:** This gentleman's name was Cockburn;—he met his end a few years afterwards in a very melancholy manner, while on his way to Montreal (having retired from the service). He rolled over the canoe on a dark night, and disappeared for ever!

CHAPTER IV

Mr. Fisher returned from town in the month of March; he had learnt that our opponents intended to shift the scene of operations to the Chats, (where the greater number of the Indians pass on their way going to or returning from their hunting grounds,) and were making preparations of a very extensive nature for the spring competition. The Company were not tardy in adopting such measures as were deemed the most efficient to meet them on their own terms. We understood that they had hired two *bullies* for the purpose of deciding the matter *par voie de fait*. Mr. Fisher hired two of the same description, who were supposed to be more than a match for the opposition party. On the 28th of April, 1822, our opponents set off in two large canoes, manned by eight men in each; we followed in three canoes with twenty-four men, under the command of three leaders—namely, Captain Ducharme, who had volunteered on the occasion, Mr. Lyons, a retired trader, and myself. Nothing occurred worthy of description on our passage to the Chats.

The Ottawa is at this point interrupted by a ledge of rock, which extends across its whole breadth. In forcing a passage for itself through this barrier, it is divided into several channels, which form as many beautiful cascades as they fall into the extensive basin that receives them below. On one of the islands thus formed, the natives make a portage. Here, then, we took our station close to a cascade: our opponents commenced building a hut on one side of the path, we on the other. While this operation was in progress, basilisk looks denoted the strength of feeling that pervaded the breasts of either party, but not a word was exchanged between us. Our hut was first completed, when our champion clambered aloft, and crowed defiance; three times he crowed (aloud), but no responding voice was heard from the opposite camp. This act was altogether voluntary on the part of our man, but it did not displease us, as the result convinced us that we stood on safe ground, should any violence be attempted. Our opponents were enraged at the want of spirit evinced by their men, and determined on being revenged upon *us* in a manner that showed the virulence of their animosity. A number of lumber men were making up their rafts within a short distance of us at the time, who were for the most part natives of the Emerald Isle. Paddy's "knocking down for love" is proverbial. Our opponents immediately sent them word that the Hudson's Bay Company had brought up a *bully* from Montreal who defied "the whole of the Grand River." "By my faith, does he thin," said Pat; "let us have a look at him, any how."

On the succeeding evening (after the occurrence of the circumstance above related) we were surprised to see the number of canoes that arrived at the portage from all directions. The crew of each canoe as they landed went direct to our opponents, where they appeared to be liberally supplied with spirits. Their object was sufficiently evident, as the potent agent they had employed, in a short time, produced the desired effect. Oaths and execrations were heard amid crowing and yelling. Our Canadians all took to their heels, except our noble game-cock and two others; and now the drama opened. A respectable good looking fellow stept out from the crowd, accompanied by another man, a Canadian, and advancing to our champion, asked him "if he would not sell his feathers" (his hat being decorated with them). It is unnecessary to state the reply. An altercation ensued, and blows would undoubtedly have succeeded, had I not then interfered. I invited the stranger to my tent, and having opened my *garde de vin*, produced some of the good things it contained. A little conversation with my guest, proved him to be a shrewd sensible man; and when I explained the nature of our dispute with our rivals, he comprehended in an instant the object they had in view in circulating the reports which induced him and others to assemble at the portage. The consanguinity of the sons of Erin and Caledonia was next touched upon, and the point settled to our mutual satisfaction; in short, my brother Celt and I parted as good friends as half-an-hour's acquaintance and a bottle of wine could make us. At the conclusion of our interview he departed, and meeting our champion, cordially shook him by the hand; then addressing his companions, remarked, "This, my lads, is a quarrel between the traders, in which we have no right to interfere at all; for my own part, I am very much obliged to the jintlemin on both sides o' the road, for traiting me so jintaily; but Jack Hall shall not be made a tool of by anybody whatsumdever."

Jack Hall embarked with his crew, and was soon afterwards followed by the others. Both parties were thus again in their previous positions, and a little tact saved us from the fatal consequences that might have ensued, had their villainous design proved successful. The daring insult was keenly felt by us all, and accordingly one of our trio despatched a message to the only individual of the opposite party who had any pretension to the title of gentleman, soliciting the pleasure of his company to take the air next morning. The invitation was accepted. Our party kept the appointment, and remained for two hours on the ground, awaiting the arrival of their *friends*; but the friends allowed them the sole enjoyment of the morning air.

A few days afterwards the natives began to make their appearance, and scenes of a revolting nature were of frequent occurrence. Rum and brandy flowed in streams, and dollars were scattered about as if they had been of no greater value than pebbles on the beach. The expenses incurred by both parties were very great; but while this lavish expenditure seriously affected the resources of the petty traders, the coffers of the Company were too liberally filled to be sensibly diminished by such outlay. Nevertheless, the natives would not dispose of their furs until they reached the village.

We remained at the portage until the 7th of June, when the natives having all passed, we embarked, and arrived at the lake on the 10th, where we were shocked to learn that our Bourgeois2 had had a very narrow escape from the treachery of an Iroquois during our absence, the particulars of which were thus related to us. Mr. Fisher had advanced a sum to this scoundrel two years before, and seeing him pass his door the ensuing spring after the debt had been contracted, with his furs, which he carried to our opponents, he watched his return, and calling him in, demanded payment; an insolent reply was the return for his kindness, which so much exasperated him, that he kicked him out in presence of several other Indians. The insult was not forgotten. Soon after his arrival this spring, he sent for Mr. Fisher, who complied with the invitation, expecting payment of his debt. The moment he entered the house, however, he discovered that he had been inveigled. The Indian stood before him, his face painted, and a pistol in his hand, which he presented. In an instant Mr. Fisher bared his breast, and staring his enemy fiercely in the face, exclaimed, "Fire, you black dog! What! did you imagine you had sent for an old woman?"

Mr. Fisher's knowledge of the Indian character saved his life; had he betrayed the slightest symptom of fear, he was a dead man; but the undaunted attitude he assumed staggered the resolution of the savage; a new bias seemed to operate on his mind, probably through a feeling of respect for the determined courage displayed by his intended victim. He could not brace his nerves to a second effort; his hand dropped listlessly by his side; his gaze was fixed on Mr. Fisher for a moment; then dashing the pistol violently on the ground, he beckoned him to withdraw.3

Immediately after the close of the spring trade, the most formidable of our opponents *hinted* that he might be induced to quit the field; a negotiation was accordingly opened with him, which soon terminated in a favourable issue, on very advantageous terms to the retiring party.

The solitary being who remained behind was thus thrown upon his own resources, and his efforts to maintain the unequal contest unaided, were so feeble and ineffectual, that the Company might be said to hold a monopoly of the fur-trade at this period; but thereafter they paid dearly for their triumph, as further sacrifices had yet to be made ere they could enjoy it in quiet. A Canadian merchant, in easy circumstances, who dwelt opposite to the village, having learned the advantageous terms obtained by the petty traders from the Company, addressed a very polite note to Mr. Fisher, stating his intention to try his fortune as a trader, but that he would have no objection to postpone the attempt for five years, provided the Company would allow him 150*l*. per annum, during that period. The proposal was submitted to Mr. Thane, who laconically replied, "Let him do his worst, and be ...." Accordingly, St. Julien immediately commenced operations. He hired one end of an Indian house, which he fitted up as a trader's shop: Fisher hired the other end. St. Julien then removed to another: Fisher occupied the other end of that house also. St. Julien next rented a *whole* house: Fisher purchased a house, placed it upon rollers, and wheeled it directly in front of that of his rival, rearwards, scarcely leaving sufficient room for one person to pass between the premises. This caused great amusement to the Indians; not so to St. Julien, who had not anticipated so excessive a desire on the part of any of the Company's officers for so close an intimacy; and at the end of six weeks he took his departure without pay or pension from the Company.

In the course of this summer our Algonquins received a visit from a party of Ottawas, (this tribe occupies the hunting grounds in the vicinity of Michimmakina or Makinaw, and speaks the Sauteaux language,) which created considerable alarm in the village, as they came for the purpose of demanding satisfaction for the murder of one of their tribe, which had been perpetrated two years before by an Algonquin. The details of the atrocious deed were communicated to me as follows. The Ottawas and Algonquins, with their families, were proceeding in company to the Lake, in the spring of 1819, when being encamped in the neighbourhood of the long Sault rapid, the Algonquin sprang upon his unsuspecting companion, and cleft his skull with his tomahawk, without the least apparent provocation; then dragging the body to the water's edge, he cut it up into small pieces, and threw them in. He next despatched the woman, and mutilated her body in the same savage manner, having first committed the most horrible barbarity on her person; (the recital of which curdled my blood; and yet our Christianized (?) Algonquins laughed heartily on hearing it!) The demon in human form, with the yet reeking tomahawk raised over the heads of his wife and children, made them swear that they would never divulge the horrid deed; but they did disclose it; and it was from the wife the tale of horror was elicited. The object of the Ottawas was not revenge. Compensation to the full estimated value of the lives of a man and woman was all they demanded; and that they received to an amount that far exceeded their expectations. Had the murderer been in the village the chiefs declared they would have given him up; but they had already delivered him over to the proper authorities, and he was then in prison waiting his sentence.

It has been already mentioned, that the Company had assumed the outstanding debts of the petty traders. When the accounts were closed this autumn, the aggregate amount of liabilities due to the Company exhibited the enormous sum of seventy-two thousand dollars—not a shilling of that sum has ever been repaid.

Soon after the departure of the natives for the interior, I was notified of my appointment to the charge of the Chats post. My friend Mac also received marching orders; and after parting with him I took leave of the Lake of Two Mountains on the 20th of August.

> **Footnote 2:** The term Bourgeois is used for Master throughout the Indian country.
>
> **Footnote 3:** At that period some of the Iroquois made good hunts, trapping beaver along the main rivers and outskirts of the Algonquin lands.

CHAPTER V

I arrived at the Chats on the 26th of August, 1822. As we approached the establishment, the crew struck up a song which soon attracted the notice of its only inmate; a tall gaunt figure, who was observed moving toward the landing-place, where it remained stationary. With the exception of this solitary being, no sign of animation was perceptible. We landed, and found the recluse to be the gentleman whom I was to succeed. The men belonging to the post were at the time employed elsewhere; fire-arms were therefore discharged, to summon them to return. An old interpreter and two men, constituting the force at this station, soon made their appearance. Such an uncommon event as an *arrival* seemed to produce an exhilarating effect upon them. Immediately after my landing the charge was made over to me; and on the following day my predecessor, Mr. Macdonald, took his departure, leaving me to the fellowship of my own musings, which for a time assumed but sombre hues; but I was then young, and the hopes and aspirations of an ardent mind threw a halo around the gloomy path that lay before me, and resting upon the bright spots that glimmered in the distant background, concealed from my view the toils and miseries I had to experience in the intermediate passage.

On assuming the responsibility of this post, I found myself in a position which gratified my vanity. I was Bourgeois of the Chats; had an interpreter and two men subject to my orders; and could make such arrangements as my own inclinations dictated, without the surveillance of a superior. I was, in fact, master of my own time and of my own actions; could fiddle when I pleased, and dance when I had a mind with my own shadow; no person here dared to question my actions.

About the beginning of September the natives began to pass for the interior, and to my great surprise appeared to be in want of further supplies, although they had left the Lake amply provided with everything necessary. Some of them took advances here again to a considerable amount. I learned from them that a petty trader who had just then sprung into existence, intended to establish a couple of posts in the interior of the district—(this post being subject to the Lake of Two Mountains.) This was rather an unpleasant piece of intelligence, and quite unexpected by my superiors or myself. I despatched a messenger to head-quarters to give the alarm, and was soon joined by a reinforcement of men conducted by a junior clerk and an interpreter. Preparations were then made to follow up this new competitor the moment he appeared. He did not allow us to remain long in suspense. A few days afterwards his party was observed passing in two canoes; our people were immediately in their wake, and I remained with but one man and the old interpreter during the winter. I had only two Indian hunters to attend to; one in the immediate vicinity of the post, the other about three days' journey distant. Late in autumn I was gratified by a visit from the superintendent of the district, who expressed himself perfectly satisfied with my arrangements. As soon as the river *set fast* with ice, I resolved on paying a visit to my more remote customer, and assumed the snow-shoes for the first time. I set out with my *only* man, leaving the old interpreter sole occupier of the post. My man had visited the Indian on several occasions during the previous winter, and told me that he usually halted at a Chantier,4 on the way to his lodge. We arrived late in the evening at the locality in question, and finding a quantity of timber collected on the ice, concluded that the *shanty* must be close at hand. We accordingly followed the lumber-track until we reached the hut which had formerly afforded such comfortable accommodation to my companion. Great was our disappointment, however, to find it now tenantless, and almost buried in snow. I had made an extraordinary effort to reach the spot in the hope of procuring good quarters for the night, and was now so completely exhausted by fatigue that I could proceed no further. The night was dark, and to make our situation as cheerless as possible, it was discovered that my companion had left his "fire-works" behind—a proof of his inexperience. Under these circumstances our preparations were necessarily few. Having laid a few boughs of pine upon the snow, we wrapped ourselves up in our blankets, and lay down together. I passed the night without much rest; but my attendant—a hardy Canadian—kept the wild beasts at bay by his deep snoring, until dawn. I found myself completely benumbed with cold; a smart walk, however, soon put the blood in circulation, and ere long we entered a shanty where we experienced the usual hospitality of these generous folks. Here we borrowed a "smoking-bag," containing a steel, flint, and tinder. With the aid of these desiderata in the appointments of a voyageur, we had a comfortable encampment on the following night.

The mode of constructing a winter encampment is simply this:—you measure with your eye the extent of ground you require for your purpose, then taking off your snow-shoes, use them as shovels to clear away the snow. This operation over, the finer branches of the balsam tree are laid upon the ground to a certain depth; then logs of dry wood are placed at right angles to the feet at a proper distance, and ignited by means of the "fire-works" alluded to. In such an encampment as this, after a plentiful supper of half-cooked peas and Indian corn—the inland travelling fare of the Montreal department—and a day's hard walking, one enjoys a repose to which the voluptuary reclining on his bed of down is a perfect stranger.

We reached our destination on the following day about noon, where we found but little to recompense us for our journey. Both our own people from the outpost and our opponents had already traded all the furs the Indian had to dispose of, although his supplies at the Lake of Two Mountains and at my post amounted to a sum that would have required his utmost exertions to pay. We remained that night at his lodge, and very early on the succeeding morning, started on our return. With the exception of a couple of trips I made to the inland posts, nothing disturbed the monotony of my avocations during the remaining part of the winter. Petty traders swarmed all over the country; the posts which were established in the interior to cope with them traded freely with the natives, in order to secure their furs from competitors. Thus the immense sacrifices which the Company had made to obtain a monopoly, as they imagined, yielded them no advantage whatever; and repeated defalcations on the part of the natives, induced them to curtail their advances at their principal station. The natives, however, found no difficulty in procuring their requisites in exchange for their furs, either from the posts belonging to the Company in the interior, or from the opposition; for they were, with few exceptions, of the same character as the individual already alluded to.

The Indian whom I mentioned as residing in the neighbourhood of the establishment arrived, late in autumn, from the Lake, where he could not obtain a charge of ammunition on credit. I supplied all his wants liberally, knowing him to be a good hunter, though a notorious rogue; and he set out for his hunting grounds, to all appearance well pleased.

In the course of the winter a Yankee adventurer opened a "grog shop," within a short distance of the depôt, who appeared to have no objection to a beaver's skin in exchange for his commodities. My Indian debtor returned in the month of March, with a tolerable "hunt," and pitched his tent midway between the post and my Yankee neighbour. I called upon the Indian immediately for payment, which he told me I should receive on the morrow. I went accordingly at the time appointed, and was annoyed to find that he had already disposed of a part of his furs for the Yankee's whiskey; and I therefore demanded payment in a tone of voice which clearly indicated that I was in earnest. To-morrow was mentioned again; but having come with the determination of being satisfied on the spot, I seized, without further ceremony, what furs remained, and throwing them out of the wigwam to my man, who was placed there to receive them, I remained within, to bear the brunt of the Indian's resentment, should he show any, until my man had secured the prize. I was well prepared to defend myself, in case of any violence being offered. Nothing of the kind was attempted, however; and I took my leave, after sustaining a volley of abuse, which did me no harm. The Indian paid me a visit next morning, for the purpose of settling accounts, a small balance being due to him, which, at his own request, was paid in rum. I soon after received another visit, for nectar, on credit; this request I granted.

The visits, however, were repeated so often for the same purpose, that I at length found it advisable to give a denial, by proxy, not wishing to part on bad terms with him, if possible, on account of the spring hunt. I absented myself from the house, having instructed my interpreter how to act. I took my station in a small grove of pines, close by, watching for the appointed signal to apprise me of the departure of the Indian. My attention was suddenly arrested by most doleful cries at the house; and presently the voice of my interpreter was heard, calling me loudly by name. I ran at the top of my speed, and arrived just in time to save the life of a poor old woman, who had been making sugar in my neighbourhood. I found the father and two sons, both approaching manhood, in a complete state of nudity, dancing round the body of their victim (to all appearance dead), their bodies besmeared with blood, and exulting in the barbarous deed they had committed. My interpreter informed me, that as soon as they observed the old woman approaching the house, the Christian father told his sons that now was the time to take revenge for the death of their brother, whose life had been destroyed by this woman's "bad medicine." We drove the wretches away, and carried the miserable woman into the house; and so dreadfully bruised and mangled were her head and face, that not the least trace of her features could be distinguished. At the end of a month she recovered sufficiently to crawl about. Her son passed in the spring, with an excellent hunt. When I related to him the manner his mother had been treated by the Indians, and the care I had taken of her, he coolly replied that he was sure they were bad Indians. "It was very charitable of you," said he, "to have taken so much care of the old woman. Come to my wigwam next winter, and I shall trade with you, and treat you well." In the meantime every skin he had went to our opponents, although he was deeply indebted to the Company.

Footnote 4: The hut used by the lumbermen, and the root of the well-known "shanty."

CHAPTER VI

A large canoe arrived from Montreal about the latter end of June, by which I received orders to proceed to Fort Coulonge, situated about eighty miles higher up the Ottawa, to relieve the person then in charge of that post. I accordingly embarked in the same canoe, accompanied by my young friend Mr. MacDougal, who joined me last autumn, and who kindly volunteered to proceed along with me to my destination. This canoe was under the charge of people hired for the trip, and directed by the bowsman, or guide. I soon discovered that I was considered merely as a piece of live lumber on board. My companion and myself were reduced to the necessity of cooking our own victuals, or of going without them. We pitched our tent as best we could, and packed it up in the morning without the slightest offer of assistance from the crew.

No incident worthy of notice occurred until we reached the Grand Calumet Portage, the longest on the Ottawa River. The crew slept at the further end of the portage, whither the canoe and part of the cargo had been carried during the day, and we pitched our tent there also in the usual awkward manner. The weather was very fine in the evening, but soon after nightfall a tremendous storm burst upon us: our tent was blown about our ears in an instant. "We endeavoured to compose ourselves to rest underneath, but found it impracticable. We then attempted to pitch it anew, but our strength and ingenuity were not sufficient for the purpose. We tried afterwards to find shelter under the canoe (the rain pouring in torrents), but the crew were already in possession, and so closely packed, that not an inch was unoccupied. Thus baffled on every hand, we passed the night completely exposed to the "pelting of the pitiless storm," learning a lesson of practical philosophy which I have not yet forgotten.

We arrived at Fort Coulonge early the next day, when a portly old gentleman, bearing a paunch that might have done credit to an Edinburgh baillie, came puffing down to the landing-place to receive us. We soon discovered that Mr. Godin was only "nominally" in charge of the establishment, for that his daughter, a stout, masculine-looking wench, full thirty summers blown, possessed what little authority was required for the management of affairs.

We arrived on Wednesday. The father proposed setting out for Montreal on Friday; the daughter objected the ill luck of the day: it was finally determined that they should embark on Thursday, however late. The necessary preparations were immediately commenced under her ladyship's superintendence, and being completed late in the evening, they embarked, leaving me perfectly alone. The contracts with the men had just expired, which I proposed to renew, but the answer from one and all was, "I shall follow my bourgeois." This was the result of the old gentleman's arrangements (having been ordered off contrary to his wishes), and which might have been anticipated by those who appointed me to the situation; but it would have been derogatory to the exalted rank of their highnesses to bestow any consideration on such trivial matters as related to the comfort or convenience of a paltry apprentice! Their neglect, however, might have been attended on this occasion with serious consequences to the Company's interests, as I had never seen any of the Indians of that quarter before, and knew very little of their mode of trading. It was a fortunate circumstance for myself that I understood the language sufficiently well to converse with the natives, otherwise my situation would have been disagreeable in the extreme. I remained alone until the latter end of July, when I was joined by an English lad, whom I induced by the promise of high wages to leave his former employers (lumbermen) and share my solitude.

The history of my predecessor being rather singular, a few words here regarding him may perhaps not be considered out of place. He commenced his career as a hired servant, or Voyageur, as they are termed in the country, and was thirty years of age before he knew a letter of the alphabet. Being a man possessed of strong natural parts, and great bodily strength withal, he soon distinguished himself as an under trader of uncommon tact,—his prowess as a pugilist also gave him a very decided advantage in the field of competition. Endowed with such qualifications, his services were duly appreciated by the traders, and he knew full well how to turn them to his own advantage. He served all parties alike; that is, he served each in turn, and cheated and deceived them all.

After the organization of the North-West Company, he entered their service; and returning to the same quarter, Temiscamingue, where he had wintered for his last employer, he passed the post unperceived, and falling in with a band of Indians, whom he himself had supplied the preceding autumn, told them he still belonged to the same party, and traded all their furs on the spot. The North-West Company gave him charge of a post, when his subtle management soon cleared the country of opposition.

The natives of Temiscamingue were in those times very treacherous, as they would be at this day, did they not dread the consequences; several men had been murdered by them, and they at length became exceedingly bold and daring in deeds of violence. One example is sufficient:—Godin happened, on one occasion, to remain at his post with only one man, who attended the nets,—fish being the staff of life in that quarter. Visiting them regularly every day to procure his own and his master's subsistence, his return was one morning delayed much beyond the usual time. Godin felt so anxious, that he determined on going to the fishery to learn the cause; and just as he had quitted the house with that intention, he met an Indian who had been for some time encamped in the vicinity, and asked him—

"What news?"

"I have killed a white dog this morning," was the reply.

"Indeed!" said Godin, feigning ignorance of the Indian's meaning: "Pray, to whom did he belong?"

"He was a stray dog, I believe."

Conversing with him in this strain, he threw the Indian completely off his guard, while he approached him until he was sufficiently near him for his purpose, when, raising his powerful arm, he struck the savage a blow under the ear that felled him to the ground,—he fell to rise no more. The next moment, a couple of well-disposed Indians came to inform Godin of the murder of his man, which it appeared they could not prevent. "My children," said he, with the utmost composure, "the Master of life has punished your kinsman on the spot for taking the life of a white man; he told me just now that he had killed a white dog, and had scarcely finished the sentence when he fell down dead at my feet. Feel his body, it must be still warm; examine it, and satisfy yourselves that he has suffered no violence from me, and you see that I have no weapons about me."

Godin was soon afterwards removed to Fort Coulonge, and was allowed a high salary by the North-West Company. Here he learned to read and write, and married a fair countrywoman of his own, who resided the greater part of the time in Montreal, where, to make the gentleman's establishment complete, he had the good taste to introduce his mistress. A circumstance that presents his character in its true colours made his wife acquainted with his infidelity. Writing to both his ladies at the same time, he unwittingly addressed his mistress's letter to his wife, by which she learnt, with other matters, that a present of ten prime otters had been sent to her rival. The enraged wife carried the letter to Mr. Thane, from whom, however, she met with a very different reception to what she had anticipated. After perusing the letter, he ordered her immediately out of his presence. "Begone, vile woman!" he exclaimed: "What! would you really wish to see your husband hanged?"

The Company were well aware of Godin's tricks, but winked at them on account of his valuable services. He was removed from Fort Coulonge in consequence of mismanagement, (occasioned by aberration of his mental faculties,) and was allowed by the Company to retire with a pension of 100*l.* per annum. The transcript of a public letter, addressed to Mr. Thane, will show his attainments in literature; and, with this I shall close my sketch of Mr. Godin:—

> "Monr Tane,
>
> "Cher Monr,
>
> "Vot letre ma té livie par Guiaume dean aisi qui le butin tout a bon ord le Shauvages on ben travaié set anne et bon aparans de bon retour st. anne Dieu merci je ne jami vu tant de moustique et de maragoen com il en a st anne je pens desend st anne ver le meme tan com l'anné pasé.
>
> "Je sui,
>
> "Cher Monr, &c.
>
> "JOSEPH GODIN."

The Indians attached to this post speak the Sauteux language, and are denominated "Tetes des Boules" by the French, and "Men of the Woods" by the other Indians. Although so near to priests and ministers, they are still Pagans, but are nevertheless a quiet harmless race, and excellent hunters. The greater part of them originally belonged to Temiscamingue, and were drawn to this quarter by Mr. Godin. A considerable number of Algonquins also trade here, where they pass the greater part of their lives without visiting the Lake. The people appear to me to differ in no respect from their heathen brethren, save in the very negligent observance of certain external forms of worship, and in being more enlightened in the arts of deceiving and lying.

About the middle of August, I was gratified by the arrival of Mr. Godin's interpreter, and three men, by whom I received letters from head-quarters, informing me that my neighbours of last winter intended to establish posts in this quarter also, and that I should soon be joined by a strong reinforcement of men, to enable me to cope successfully with them. We complain of solitude in the Indian forests, yet the vicinity of such a neighbour is considered the greatest evil; and instead of cherishing the feelings enjoined in the Decalogue, one hates his neighbour as the d——l, and employs every means to get rid of him.

The natives having been all supplied, had taken their departure for their hunting-grounds by the latter end of August; I then commenced making the arrangements requisite for the coming contest.

CHAPTER VII

About the middle of September, I observed a north canoe paddling in for the landing-place, having a gentleman passenger on board, who immediately on landing ordered his servant to carry his baggage up to the Fort. On his entering the house, the apparent mystery was soon unfolded. Mr. Siviright handed me a letter from Mr. Thane, conveying the agreeable Intelligence of my being superseded by the bearer,—commanding me to obey him as my bourgeois, and to conduct myself in such a manner as to give Mr. S. every satisfaction. The latter injunction I felt very little inclination to comply with at the time; in fact, the slight put upon me caused my northern blood to rise to fever heat; and in this excited frame of mind I sat down to reply to the "great man's" communication, in which I gave vent to my injured feelings in very plain language. What he may have thought of the epistle, I know not, as he never deigned to reply. It was inconsiderate in me, however, to have so acted; but prudence had not yet assumed her due influence over me.

Mr. S. had been at that time twenty-four years in the service, I only three; he had therefore a superior claim to any I could advance: but why not inform me at once that my appointment to the charge was merely temporary? This double dealing manifested a distrust of me, for which no cause could possibly be assigned: that excited my resentment, and not the circumstance of being superseded.

Towards the latter end of the month of September, our opponents made their appearance in three small canoes, while I embarked in pursuit with the same number. One of my north canoes was in charge of three men, the others contained two, counting myself as a man. Having become rather expert as an amateur voyageur, I considered myself capable of undertaking the real duty now, and accordingly volunteered my services as steersman, as no additional hand could be spared, without great inconvenience to my bourgeois. A little experience convinced me, however, that my zeal exceeded my ability. My opponent was in a light canoe, and moved, about with a celerity that my utmost exertions could not cope with; for as soon as an Indian canoe appeared, he paddled off for it; I of course attempted to compete, but generally arrived just in time to find that he had already concluded his transaction with the hunters.

We reached Black River on the third day from Fort Coulonge, where it appeared my opponent's intention to remain for some time, to await the arrival of certain Indians who were expected down by that river. I determined therefore to despatch a canoe to Fort Coulonge, to acquaint Mr. S with the particulars above related; and sent back therewith such of the property as I thought could be dispensed with at the time, as it was quite evident we could not keep up with our opponent in the portages with such a quantity of baggage as we then had, and we could obtain no information that could be depended upon as to their ultimate destination—it might be at the distance of a hundred miles, or only ten.

My messengers were but two days absent; and I was not a little mortified to learn from them, that Mr. S., instead of attending to my suggestions, not only returned all the property I had sent, but nearly an equal quantity in addition. He wrote me his reasons for doing so; but I felt assured that he had no other object in view than to show me that he was the superior, I the subordinate; and I resolved from that moment, to perform no more extra duty.

After continuing a fortnight at our encampment, we again embarked, when I ordered the third man in the large canoe into my own, and tossing my paddle down stream, took my station in the middle of my canoe. A few hours' paddling brought us to an old shanty in the island of Allumette, where, to my great joy, I perceived my opponent intended to fix his winter quarters. We accordingly commenced erecting a couple of huts, a store, and dwelling-house, in close proximity to him. This being the best season of the year for the natives to hunt, it was the interest of all parties not to molest them; and we therefore employed our time in preparing suitable accommodation for the winter.

On the completion of our arrangements, I set out, about the beginning of October, on a visit to Fort Coulonge; and on the day after my arrival there we observed a north canoe paddling slowly past, and distinguished the features of every individual on board through a telescope, but could recognise no one: however, to clear up the doubt, the interpreter was sent after them in a small canoe, with instructions to make a close scrutiny. They no sooner discovered that he was in pursuit, than they ceased paddling. After a long confabulation he learned that they were proceeding to Sault St. Marie, where they intended to settle. I passed two days with my bourgeois, and returned home, where we—our opponents and ourselves—watched each other's movements, being our only occupation until the end of November, when Mr. S. paid me a visit, which proved anything but gratifying.

He (Mr. S.) had learned from some lumbermen, that the "Settlers for the Sault Ste. Marie" were an opposition party conducted by Mr. Æneas Macdonell, my predecessor at the Chats; and that he purposed to *settle* for the winter near Lac des Allumettes. This gentleman's engagement had been cancelled at the earnest solicitation of his father, whom death had lately deprived of another son; and who now, to requite the favour granted to him by the Company, sent this son in opposition! We had barely a sufficient number of men to perform the necessary duties of the two posts already established; we were, therefore, completely at a loss to meet this emergency. Mr. S. could spare one man only from his own post, whom he brought up to me.

I embarked early next morning with one of my own men, in search of the "settler." On reaching Lac des Allumettes on the same evening, our attention was arrested by the voices of Indians, singing on an island. We immediately pulled in for the spot, and found a large camp of Algonquins, men, women and children, all in a state of intoxication; from whom I learned, though with much difficulty, the whereabouts of Macdonell's retreat. Quitting this disgusting scene as speedily as possible, we resumed our paddles, and soon afterwards discovered the opposition post. When we landed, my quondam mess-mate advanced to receive me, and, after a cordial shake of the hand, kindly invited me to pass the night with him. I gladly accepted the offer; and was not a little concerned to perceive that his preparations for winter were already complete; a circumstance which gave him a decided advantage. Happening in the course of conversation to express my surprise at seeing him in the character of an opponent, he told me that nothing could be farther from his intention than to oppose the Company. He came to this quarter for the purpose of preparing timber for the Quebec market; in provincial phrase, "to make a shanty." But I knew well enough his designs.

I started early next morning on my return, and immediately thereafter prepared a small outfit; and re-embarked next evening with five men in two canoes, leaving the interpreter in charge of the post, with one man to assist him.

Having experienced very bad weather on our way, and consequently some delay, we did not reach our new station until late in the evening of the fourth day. I immediately sent back two of the men to the interpreter, and retained three with myself, which placed me on a par with my opponent in point of numbers. But he was now ready for active operations, while I had every thing to prepare. I resolved, however, to forego every personal comfort and convenience rather than allow him to enjoy any advantage over me. I accordingly assisted in erecting a small hut, which I intended should serve for dwelling-house for myself and men, trading-shop, store and all.

A couple of days after our arrival, Macdonell was seen walking down to the water's edge with a very cautious step, accompanied by one of his men, bearing his canoe, basket fashion, on one arm, and a large bundle on the other, from which, notwithstanding his steady pace, the jumbling sound of liquor was distinctly heard.

"Holla, Mac, where are you going with your basket?"

"Why, I am going across to Herd's shanty, to get my axes ground."

"My dear fellow, how can you think of risking yourself in such a gimcrack contrivance as that? I must absolutely send a couple of my men along with you to see no accident happens to you."

Having a parcel of goods ready for emergencies of this kind, my men started in a moment, and embarked at the same time as my neighbour. I continued with my only man completing my castle; but the earth being already hard frozen, no clay could be obtained for the purpose of plastering; the interstices between the logs were therefore caulked with moss; a large aperture being left in the roof to serve the double purpose of chimney and window. I had formerly seen houses so constructed—somewhere—but let no one dare to imagine that I allude to "my own, my native land." Stones were piled up against the logs, to protect them from the fire. The timber required for floor, door, and beds, was all prepared with the axe; our building being thus rendered habitable without even going to the extent of Lycurgus' frugal laws, for the axe was our only implement.

My opponent returned in four days, having been at an Indian camp, not far distant, where both he and our people traded a considerable quantity of furs. This was our only trip by open water. As soon as the river became ice-bound, we were again in motion.

To enter into minute details of our various movements would but prove tedious; I shall therefore present a general sketch of our mode of life at this period, and such occurrences as I may consider worthy of note.

Macdonell had chosen his situation with great judgment. The majority of the Algonquins take their start from the Grand River at this place for their hunting-grounds. Some of them not being more than a day's journey distant from us, the joyful intelligence soon spread amongst them that an opposition party had been established in their neighbourhood; they accordingly flocked about us as soon as travelling became practicable on the ice, and generally brought with them the means of ensuring a friendly reception. One party came in at this early season with all their fall hunts, which they bartered for liquors and provisions, and encamped close by, enjoying themselves, until an event occurred that alarmed them so much, (being with some reason considered by them as a punishment for the wicked life they had led,) that with the utmost precipitation they struck their camp.

I was joined early in the month of January by a party of men and a clerk, whom Mr. S. had ordered, or rather "requested," from Montreal; and having, on the day of their arrival, received an invitation from one of our Algonquin chiefs to pay him a *trading* visit, I started next day, leaving Mr. Lane in charge, accompanied by two men, and reached the chief's wigwam late in the evening. As soon as I was seated, he asked me if I had not met the Matawin Indians. On my replying in the negative, he informed me that they had passed his place early in the morning, loaded with furs, and that they expressed their intention of proceeding to the post before they halted. These Indians had all been supplied by myself in autumn to a large amount; so that the intelligence acted on my nerves like an electric shock. I felt much fatigued on entering the lodge, but I now sprung to my feet, as fresh for the journey as when I had commenced it; and ordering one of my men to return with me, left the other, an experienced hand, to manage affairs with the chief.

I arrived at my post about two next morning, when I found the Indians, some at our hut, some at our opponent's, all of them approaching the climax of Indian happiness, and Mr. Lane in a state of mind bordering on distraction. Neither he nor any of the men had ever seen any of these Indians before, nor did they understand a word of the language. The Indians were honest enough, however, to give him their furs in charge till my return; reserving only a small quantity to dispose of at discretion. My arrival was soon announced at my neighbour's, and brought the whole bevy about me in an instant, only one individual remaining behind. On inquiring into the cause of his absence, his companions replied that he had fallen asleep immediately after he had supped, and that they did not wish to disturb him.

A few hours afterwards I was not a little surprised to see my neighbour entering our hut hurriedly, who addressed me thus:—

"My dear Mac, it is true we are in opposition, but no enmity exists between us. A dreadful misfortune happened in my house last night.— Come and see!"

I instantly complied with his request; proceeded to his hut, and saw the Indian who was said to be asleep, with his eyes closed—for ever; a sad spectacle, for it was evident that the death of the poor wretch had been caused by intemperance; he was found in the morning lying on his face, and his body already stiff. We were both alike involved in the same awful responsibility, for the Indians drank as much at one house as the other, though his death occurred at the establishment of the other party. The Company only permit the sale of liquors to the natives when the presence of opponents renders it an indispensable article of trade, as it is by this unhallowed traffic that the petty traders realize their greatest profit. Yet this plea of necessity, however satisfactory it may appear in a certain quarter, will not, I feel assured, be accepted in our vindication by the world, nor hereafter in our justification at that tribunal where worldly considerations have no influence. Information soon reached the camp of the calamity that had happened, which promptly silenced the clamorous mirth that prevailed; and the voice of mourning succeeded—the Indians being all in good crying trim, that is, intoxicated; for I have never seen an Indian shed a tear when sober.

No more liquor was traded; the relatives of the deceased departed with the body to the Lake of Two Mountains, and the other Indians started for their hunting-grounds—thus granting us a short respite from the arduous duties in which we had been engaged. While the Indians remained about us we never enjoyed a moment's refreshing rest, our hut being crowded with them night and day. It was at times with difficulty we could prepare our victuals, or, when cooked, command sufficient time to partake of a hasty meal, in the midst of the "living mass" that environed us. All this was extremely annoying; but other comforts must be added ere this picture of the life we then led is complete. The motions of our opponents must needs be attended to, at dawn of day; each morning every path was carefully examined, to ascertain that no one had started during night: these precautions were also punctually taken by our opponents; and every stratagem that could be devised to elude each other's vigilance put in practice, it being the "interest" of each party to reach the Indians alone.

CHAPTER VIII

When we discovered that our opponents had outwitted us, we would despatch messengers in pursuit; and I need scarcely add, the same means were resorted to by our neighbours, when inquisitive about our movements. We had now the advantage in point of numbers, being nearly two to one; yet it so happened that we seldom could perform a trip unattended; very frequently by a single man against two or three—still he got his share; for the system of trade in this quarter does not allow violent means being employed to obtain possession of the products of the hunt. The mode of procedure is this:—On entering the lodge of an Indian, you present him with a small keg of nectar, as a propitiatory offering; then, in suppliant tones, request payment of the debt he may owe you, which he probably defers to a future day—the day of judgment. If your opponent be present, you dare not open your lips in objection to the delay; for you may offend his dignity, and consequently lose all his furs. This you are aware of, and accordingly proceed to untie your pack, and exposing its contents to view, solicit him to give, at least, the preference in trade. Your opponent, on the other side of the fire-place, having also poured out his libation, imitates your example in every respect; and most probably he may secure the wife, while you engage the husband as customers.

A few weeks elapsed without the arrival of any hunters, and we were beginning to recover from the effects of our late fatigues, when a numerous band arrived from a considerable distance, and encamped on the same spot that had been occupied by those lately noticed, and the same riotous scenes were again enacted, although these new comers were fully aware of the misfortune that had already occurred in consequence of similar disgusting intemperance.

Among this band was a son of the principal sachem of the Algonquins, who was acknowledged heir apparent to his *dad's vermin,* and who assumed the airs of a man of great consequence, in virtue of his prospective dignity. The father bore a respectable character; the son was a sot. In consideration of his furs, however, I paid him some little attentions, though much against my inclination. He came one evening reeling into our hut, more than "half-seas over," having been thus far advanced on his voyage to Elysium through the insinuating influences of my opponent's "fire-water;" and seating himself on a three-legged stool, close to the fire-place, he soon began to nod; then, losing his equilibrium, ultimately fell at full length on the floor. I could not suppress a smile at sight of his copper highness's prostrate position, when springing up in a furious passion, he seized an axe, and proceeded to demolish the seat. I wrested the axe from his grasp, and reprimanded him sharply for his insolence. This exasperated him to the utmost: he swore I was in league with the stool to insult him; but that he should be revenged on us both before morning. Uttering these menaces, he set out for the camp.

It so happened that a strong party of men arrived on that evening from Fort Coulonge with supplies, and were huddled together with myself and my men, all under the same roof. The greater part of them lay down to rest; but a few still continued the vigil, indulging in the favourite luxury of smoking, and chatting about the enjoyments of "Mont-rial,"—when, all of a sudden, the dread-inspiring war-whoop echoed through our little hut; the next instant the door flew off its wooden hinges, and fell with a crash on the floor, exhibiting to view the person of the Indian, standing on the threshold, holding a double-barrelled gun in his hand, with blackened face and his eyes flashing fire.

The men had now all started to their feet, as well as myself. The moment the eyes of the savage fell upon me, in the midst of the crowd, he brought the piece to bear upon me, or at least attempted to do so; but I sprang upon him with a bound, and beat the muzzle down; instantly the discharge followed: we then struggled for the possession of the gun, which I quickly wrested from his grasp; and, applying the butt end of it "gently" to his ear, laid him sprawling at my feet.

On the discharge of the gun, I heard a voice calling out, "Mon Dieu!" and another, in a plaintive tone, exclaiming, "Ah mon garçon!" This was all I heard distinctly, when every voice joined in one cry, "Tueons le crapaud;" and presently the wretched Indian was kicked and cuffed by as many as could press round him. I called on them to desist—as well have spoken to the wind!—not a soul heeded my orders. At length one of them observed, "What occasion is there for more beating of him—the black dog is dead enough."

I looked about for the person whom I supposed to have been wounded, in vain—the whole mass was in motion. As soon as the tumult had subsided, however, I was glad to find that no one had received any serious injury; the ball had grazed the thigh of a youth (who had arrived from Montreal on a visit to his father), and lodged in a log of the building.

The uproar occasioned by the men soon brought the Indians from the camp about the hut; and perceiving the apparently lifeless body stretched on the floor, they raised a yell that was reverberated by the surrounding hills. "Revenge! revenge!" shouted every savage present. We mustered too strong, however, to permit their threats being put into execution without great hazard to themselves; which fact pressed itself so powerfully on their minds, that for the present they discreetly vented their rage in abuse, and returned to their quarters. Satisfied by the feeble beating of the Indian's pulse that the vital spark was not extinct, I would not allow his kinsmen to remove him. Towards morning, recovering the use of speech, he inquired, in a voice scarcely audible, if he "had shed the blood of a white man?" I replied in the affirmative. "Then," said he, "it would have been better had you despatched me at once, for I shall certainly be hanged."

With the view of pacifying the natives, I deemed it advisable to represent the young man's wound as very severe, and exercised my wits to give my representation the semblance of truth. I caused the young man's leg to be carefully bandaged; and, luckily, happening to have a fresh beaver in the house, the bandage was speedily besmeared with its blood, and the sound patient placed in bed, with instructions how to act his part. The Indians returned early on the following morning to inquire after their young chief, and being all perfectly sober, I descanted on the calamity of the previous night, describing *my* young man's case to be of such a serious nature as to induce the apprehension that death, or at least amputation of the limb, would be the consequence. In confirmation of the veracity of this statement, the afflicted leg was exposed to view, while the patient's groans, which impressed on the minds of the bystanders the conviction of the pain he endured, prevented too close a scrutiny.

"Alas!" they exclaimed, "it is all very true. Wagh! this is indeed a sad business; but the bad fire-water is to blame for it all."

My stratagem had succeeded. Most of the natives acknowledged the justice of the punishment inflicted on their young chief, who had a brother present, however, whose sullen countenance betrayed the vindictive feelings in his breast, although he maintained a profound silence.

The Fort Coulonge party started early next day, dragging their wounded companion on a sled, until they were out of sight. The relatives of the chief removed him to the camp, where he soon recovered. All the other Indians took their departure on the day following the affray. Shortly afterwards we were favoured with a visit from one whose hunting-grounds bordered on Rice Lake, a distance of 150 miles. I had advanced this Indian all the supplies he required previous to Mr. Siviright's arrival, which formed a pretty large amount. On examining the books, he animadverted upon the advance in terms of disapprobation, as being very imprudent to risk so much with an

Indian. Most gratified and happy was I then to learn from the hunter that he had sufficient to liquidate the debt, and nearly as much more to trade. On making out his requisition for the latter purpose, it was found that four sleds at least would be required for the transport of all the property. To employ this number in one direction, however, would leave my neighbour at liberty to prosecute his views in another quarter without the necessary attendance. Still, I determined on risking a point, and securing at all hazards the valuable prize now offered. Obtaining a *piece* at the sacrifice of a *pawn* is considered good play.

I proceeded accordingly with the Indian, accompanied by four men, all with heavily laden sleds, with a pack of goods strapped over my shoulders weighing eighty pounds. Macdonell did not follow, as the Indian gave him no encouragement. We reached the Indian's lodge on the eleventh day from the post, when the abundant display of furs I beheld gave assurance of being amply remunerated for my trip. There were eleven packs of beaver piled upon a scaffold, besides some others, amounting to at least 600*l*. sterling. My hospitable customer detained me two days with him to partake of his good cheer. After settling accounts with him, together with payment of the sum he owed, seven of the eleven packs were placed in my possession, with which I started on my return, as proud as if I had been advanced to a share in the Company.

We arrived at the post after an absence of twenty-five days; and I was mortified to learn that my substitute had most stupidly bungled affairs. A number of Indians had come in during my absence who were considered our best friends, and entering our hut without noticing our opponent, threw down their bundles, thereby clearly indicating, according to the usual custom, their intention of trading with one party only. On the other hand, should they leave a bundle at the door, it shows that they intend to divide its contents between two parties. With these particulars the interpreter's experience rendered him perfectly well acquainted, but he "cau'd na be fasht."

It is customary when the Indians arrive, to present each with a pipe, a plug of tobacco, and, though last, not least in their estimation, "a dram." The usual *politesse* was expected as a matter of course on this occasion. Seeing it was not forthcoming, the Indians demanded it. They were answered that no instructions had been left to that effect.

"Very well," said they, "we shall soon find it elsewhere." And away they went.

Macdonell received them with open arms. His reception not only induced them to trade every skin they had brought with them, but they also invited him to their camp; and he consequently returned with his own and his men's sleds laden with furs.

I learnt all these particulars from himself; for he and I were on as good terms as the nature of our occupation and our relative positions would admit. I was, moreover, made acquainted through him that the Indians had expressed regret at my absence, and that an immense quantity of "beaver" still remained at their camp.

The spring was now fast approaching, the ice so bad as to render travelling dangerous, and but little snow on the ground. Still, I determined on paying a visit to these Indians, in order to retrieve the loss, if possible, sustained through the mismanagement of the interpreter. They might yet be in want of some supplies, poor fellows; and we were all so anxious they should want for nothing we could spare for their accommodation;—we, therefore, good, humane souls, supplied them even at the hazard of our lives.

CHAPTER IX

I set off on this trip accompanied by another interpreter recently sent from Montreal, and one of my men, all with heavy burdens on our backs, the season not allowing the use of sledges. The second day we arrived at an Indian lodge about half-way to the Bear's Camp, where I learned that our opponent at the lower outpost had given our people the slip, but had been induced to return from the supposition that the extensive swamp in his way was impassable, being so inundated as to present the appearance of a lake. Urged on, however, by youthful ardour and ambition, I determined to make at least one attempt ere I relinquished the enterprise; although I acknowledge that the idea of overcoming difficulties deemed insurmountable by an opponent, had as much to do with the resolution as the desire of doing my duty. Followed by my men, I accordingly plunged in, along the margin of the marsh; the water reached our middle, but we found it to decrease in depth as we proceeded, though never below the knee. The water being very cold, our legs soon became quite benumbed; nevertheless we moved onward. A certain passage in history occurred to my mind, which records the perseverance of a great man in a like situation. I too persevered, though with a different object in view. We all have our hobbies. I waded for furs, he for glory. We occasionally met with large trunks of trees as we proceeded, on which we mounted, and restored the circulation to our limbs by stamping upon them; and thus, after five or six hours' painful exertion we reached dry land, where a rousing fire and a hearty breakfast made us soon forget the miseries of the swamp.

We reached the old *bear's den* next evening, who, with his party, expressed much surprise to see me at such a season, and in recompense for my exertions, "traded"5 every article of goods I had.

There were here seven Indians, who, notwithstanding the frequent visits that had been paid them, in the course of the winter, by the people of the lower posts, had still upwards of forty packs of beaver. I got one pack, with which I set off on my return, pleased enough. We found the water in the swamp so far subsided as to permit an easy passage; but the ice on the Grand River was so much worse that we were compelled to travel in the woods the greater part of the way.

On arriving at the post, I found the opposition party in active preparation for their departure, Macdonell having received orders from his father to that effect. He embarked as soon as the navigation became practicable. Opponent as he was, I experienced some painful sensations at parting with him; but soon had the *consolation* to see our opponent at the lower post occupy his place,—a measure which he ought to have adopted at a much earlier period, as even then it gave him a much better chance for a share of the spring trade than below, where he might be said to be placed between two fires. His removal, however, enabled us to concentrate our whole strength against him, so that he could not move a foot without a strong party at his heels. Thus circumstanced, he chose to await the arrival of the natives quietly at his post, and we were happy to follow his example.

The spring passed in a happy state of quiescence, which was scarcely disturbed by the arrival of the Indians, who, this year, had all taken a fancy to visit their ghostly fathers at the Lake,6 and had, consequently, no time to spend with us; some intending to get married, some having children to be baptized, and some carrying their dead, in order that the last sacred rites for the benefit of their departed spirits might be performed upon them. A few *têtes de boules* remained for some time, but under so strict a surveillance that they could seldom communicate with our opponents without being observed, and the discovery subjected them to some chastisement.

I shall here relate a circumstance that occurred at this time, as an example of the cunning of the Indians in devising plans to evade us. Soon after their arrival, an old squaw brought to our house several casseaux7 of sugar, and pointing out one, which she said was left open for immediate consumption, said she would return for it presently. She came next day and took the casseaux down to the tent of the Algonquin chief, who had passed the spring close by, and was now building a canoe, preparatory to his departure for the Lake. Soon after I went to have a chat with the chief, and found only his squaw at home. I observed the casseau, and asked for what purpose it was brought there. "Mine hostess" smiled, and answered, "You ought to know everything about it, when it has just quitted your house and passed the night with you. You whites pretend to be very cunning," she continued, "but when an Indian, or even an old squaw tries to cheat you, your 'white' knowledge is no match for her. Now look into that casseau, Anamatik,8 and see what is in it."

I looked, and found, instead of sugar, a very valuable bundle of furs.

"What do you think of the sugar?"

"Oh, it is very fine indeed; so much finer than any that I have, that I must take it along with me."

"Your white neighbour will be angry with you, for it is left here for him."

"Let him come to my house if he wants any."

I set off with my prize, and as soon as it was deposited in a place of safety, took up a favourable position to watch my opponent, whom I soon perceived making for the tent with long and rapid strides. I could not help laughing heartily at the idea of his disappointment, when told what had happened. The "fair deceiver," to whom the bone of contention had belonged, soon made her appearance with downcast looks, humbly entreating payment for her furs, and I paid her the full amount, after lecturing her severely on the treachery of her conduct *in doing "what she willed with her own."*

My opponent embarked on the 10th June, and I immediately followed him to the lower post, which he left in charge of one man, and then set off for Montreal. I kept him company as far as Fort Coulonge, where I met with a very friendly reception from my bourgeois,—the collected trade of the different posts having far exceeded his most sanguine expectations. He set out for Montreal with returns of the value of 5,000*l*. sterling, and left me in charge for the summer at Fort Coulonge, and Mr. Lane at the outpost. Only one family of Algonquins passed the summer inland,—the same miscreants that had nearly murdered the old woman at the Chats; a deed which I had neither forgotten, nor could divest myself of the feelings of indignation it had awakened in my breast.

In the course of the summer, the interpreter of the post being in want of some paddles, employed this exemplary father to make them, and paid for them in rum. The quantity was so small, however, that it only had the effect of exciting their thirst, and they returned early in the night for more, which was peremptorily refused. The doors were bolted, and we retired to rest; but rest they were determined we should not have that night; and they continued knocking at the doors and windows, and bawling out at the top of their lungs, "Rum,—more rum!" until daylight next morning. I rose very early, in not the best humour possible, and taking the key of the store in my hand—I know not for what purpose—went out, and was followed by the Indian, still demanding more rum. I told him he should have none from me. "But I must have some." "Then you shall go elsewhere for it;" and without more ado, I turned him out, pushing him with some violence from the door. He fell on his face on the platform that ran in front of the building, and leaving him there to recover his footing at leisure, I returned towards the dwelling-house; but had scarcely reached the end of the platform, when the yell of defiance, "Hee-eep, hoo-aw!" resounded in my ears. I instantly wheeled round, and found myself face to face with the Indian. The old villain attempted to collar me, but, enraged to madness, I now grappled with him, and with all my might hurled him from the platform to the ground.

I stood for a moment hesitating whether I should strike him while down, but had little time to deliberate,—the savage was again on his legs. He rushed towards a gun that stood against a fur-press hard by; I instantly comprehended his intention, and finding a stick at hand, in the twinkling of an eye, I struck him a blow that laid him senseless on the ground. Being scarcely aware of what I was doing, I was about to repeat the blow, when I found the uplifted weapon seized from behind. It was Primeau, my interpreter, who addressed me in a soothing tone, telling me I had already "done for" the Indian.

This startling announcement restored me to reason. Was I indeed guilty of the blood of a fellow-creature? The thought chilled me with horror. I dashed the stick to the ground. It was instantly picked up by one of his three sons, whom the noise of the scuffle had now brought all up; brandishing it aloft, he aimed a blow at my head, which I parried with my arm, the limb dropping senseless to my side. My men, however, were now on the spot to defend me, and a fierce scuffle took place between them and the Indian's sons. Had they been the stronger party on this occasion, my fur-trading career would have terminated that morning. They, however, got a sound drubbing; while their wretched father, who had been the cause of the disturbance, lay unheeded and unconscious on the spot where he had fallen, not exhibiting the least sign of life.

A place of temporary accommodation being prepared by his family, he was borne thither on a blanket, and I retired to my quarters in a state of mind not easy to be described. Soon after, the interpreter came in with a message from the Indians, entreating me to come and advise with them touching the manner in which they should dispose of their father's body. I went, and just as I stepped within the camp, to the astonishment of all present, the dead man sprang upon his feet. Seeing me at his side, he exclaimed, "You shall have cause to repent this!" The words were scarcely out of his mouth, when he sank down again, and for a period of six weeks after he remained as helpless as an infant. He was subsequently carried down to the Lake of Two Mountains, where he recovered from the effects of this castigation, to die, two years after, in a fit of drunkenness.

Footnote 5: *Anglicè,*—bought.

Footnote 6: Of the Two Mountains.

Footnote 7: Packages made of bark.

Footnote 8: My Indian cognomen.

CHAPTER X

Mr. Siviright arrived about the latter end of August, accompanied by another junior clerk, and a few days afterwards the opposition were seen passing. I embarked with my fellow-scribe, and arrived next day at the lower outpost, when I was much disappointed to find my old interpreter, whom I had with me at the Chats, in the service of our opponents. He was my Indian tutor, and took every pains, not only to teach me the language, but to initiate me in the mysteries of the trade, in which he was justly considered an adept. Our opponents offered him a high salary, which he would not accept until he had previously made a tender of his valuable services to the Company, whom he had faithfully served for a period of thirty years and upwards. He requested a small addition to his salary, which was refused.

My regard for the worthy old man, however, was not in the least diminished by the circumstance of his being in opposition. Père Duchamp and I had still our friendly *tête-à-tête* whenever we had an opportunity. The autumn passed without any incident having occurred worthy of note, I and my opponent being occupied in the usual way,—watching each other night and day, chasing each other, and circumventing each other when we could.

Late in the month of October, I was surprised to observe a couple of middle-sized canoes, deeply laden, put ashore at our opponent's, where the crews, five in number, passed the night. Next morning, as soon as they were gone, I called on my old friend, who happened to be alone at the time, to inquire about his visitors.

He demurred for a little, and at length said: "For your sake, and to you only, would I disclose the secret of these people's object and destination. They called at Fort Coulonge yesterday, and gave themselves out for a party of hunters, bound for the Temiscamingue quarter;—they are a party of Iroquois, supplied with a valuable assortment of goods for trade, and their destination is Lac de la Vieille, in the very centre of the Algonquin hunting-grounds."

This was a most important piece of intelligence: some of these Indians had been supplied at Fort Coulonge, some at my post, and all of them were deeply indebted at the Lake of Two Mountains. I passed the day in the anxious expectation of seeing Mr. S., or at least receiving instructions from him with reference to these people. No one coming, I resolved to proceed to Fort Coulonge, and communicate *viva voce* the information I had received.

Late in the evening, I embarked in a small canoe, with two men, and reached the Fort at early dawn; and rousing Mr. S. from his slumbers, I at once announced the object of my visit.

"Well," said he, "this requires consideration: retire to rest, and I shall think about it."

I retired accordingly, and slept till breakfast-time, when the subject was discussed; and his decision was, that I should send one of the two young men who were at my post in pursuit of the Iroquois, with instructions to follow them up, until the season should be so far advanced as merely to admit of his return by open water, unless the Iroquois pitched their tent before then.

I volunteered myself to go after them with an outfit; but no; it would be dividing our forces, thereby allowing an advantage to our more formidable opponents; besides, we had not much to apprehend from the Iroquois with their trifling means. "*Très bien*," I said to myself, and set off on my return forthwith. I of course lost no time in executing the orders I had received. My bourgeois had his opinion of the matter, and I had mine; I knew that the Iroquois, when left to themselves, would make their own prices for their goods, and thus, even with the small outfit they had, fleece the Indians of the principal part of their furs.

Among the Indians whom I had supplied, was an individual whose advances amounted to a heavy sum. I felt extremely anxious about him, and resolved to pay him a visit as soon as travelling was practicable; meantime, Swanston, who had been in pursuit of the Iroquois, returned from his disagreeable voyage on the 28th November, having learned nothing more than we already knew.

I set off the next day, ostensibly on a visit to Mr. S., but really with the intention of starting from his post on my intended "derouine,"[9] arrived at Fort Coulonge among the drift ice, and on the 1st December started, accompanied by the interpreter Primeau and another man, all of us with heavy burdens on our backs. This proved the most toilsome trip I had yet undertaken; the smaller lakes only were passable on the ice, and the rivers were nearly all open. The difficulties we thus encountered necessarily retarded our progress, and occupied so much more time than we had calculated upon, that our provisions were nearly consumed by the time we reached the first Indian camp, where we expected to procure a guide to conduct us to the party we were in search of. We succeeded in hiring a young man, but we only obtained a small supply of flour, the Indians having no other kind of provision to spare.

Three days travelling brought us to the borders of the Indian's lands, where we soon discovered one of his early winter encampments; had we been a few days sooner we could have easily traced him from this spot, but the snow, which had recently fallen to a great depth, had nearly obliterated the marks he had left behind him.10 My interpreter, accustomed to "tracking," followed the *scent* for two days; our guide, discontented with the short allowance, gave no assistance, till coming to an extensive "brulé,"11 he was completely *at fault,* as no marks of any kind could be discovered.

Our situation was now extremely critical; we were reduced to one solitary meal of flour and water per diem, and but a few handfuls of this poor fare remained; to return by the way we came was out of the question, to proceed to the post was in truth our only alternative, and none of us was sufficiently acquainted with that part of the country to be sure of finding it; while the Indian, positively refusing to keep us company any longer, turned back, and left us to get out of our difficulties as we best could.

The interpreter proposed that another attempt should be made to find the Indian's encampment, and volunteered to go alone; this proved the poor fellow's zeal, but he returned to our encampment next morning unsuccessful; we therefore resolved to go back, and, finding our way without much difficulty for a couple of days, we reached the upper end of a long portage leading to the Ottawa River, where we encamped late in the evening, and supped on the *hope* of getting to the post next forenoon.

We started early in the morning, the Canadian leading, and about noon fell on fresh snow-shoe tracks—the tracks, we supposed, of some of our people who had come to seek us; and feeling assured that our sufferings would terminate with the day, we pursued our route with renovated vigour and speed; when lo! our encampment of the preceding night came in view, the excitement of our minds having prevented us from discerning our mistake, as we might have done, sooner. The sun was still high, but the circumstance of the encampment being already prepared, induced us to put up there again for the night. It was a sad disappointment, and I felt it as such, though I affected a gaiety that was far from my heart; while with downcast looks and heavy hearts my poor fellows betook themselves to rest at a very early hour.

Next morning we set off determined to be more cautious; the mistake of the previous day was ascribed to the sound of a high cascade at the head of the rapid, which we had mistaken for another considerably farther down; our Canadian still acted as guide—the blind leading the blind—and after two hours' walk we fell upon our own tracks again;—the poor fellow had yielded so completely to despair, that he walked about mechanically, scarcely knowing or caring whither he went; he was therefore ordered to the rear, and Primeau succeeded as leader. We saw nothing more of our tracks, but encamped in the evening with much the same prospects as before. I felt extremely weak, having carried Primeau's pack along with my own, as the old man could scarcely move when beating the track in the deep snow. Having a few fresh beaver skins, we cut off the thicker parts about the head and legs, and made a *bouillon* of them, which we drank, and then turned in.

In the morning it became a subject of serious debate what direction we should proceed in; the sky, however, having been clear the preceding evening, I observed the sun setting, and determined in my own mind the proper course; both my companions differed from me, but readily agreed to follow me. I therefore took the lead, and was so fortunate as to discover an old track, soon after leaving our encampment, which we followed until it brought us in sight of the Grand River—the long looked-for object of our fast failing hopes. Tears of joy burst from my eyes, as I beheld before me the wide expanse of the noble stream: although covered with ice and divested of the beauties of summer, it never appeared more lovely to me. We reached the post after night-fall; opening the door cautiously, I threw in my snow-shoes, then bolting in myself, was gratified with the sight of a table garnished with the best things the country afforded, which my two friends had prepared for their Christmas dinner; the sight, however, was all that prudence allowed us for the present to enjoy, our long abstinence rendering it necessary to confine ourselves, for a time, to a very weak diet.

Next day I despatched a messenger to Fort Coulonge with the narrative of my adventures; and as soon as my strength was sufficiently recruited I set off again, accompanied by a *tête de boule* as my guide, who led us direct to the camp of the Indian I had so long been in search of; where I had the mortification to learn, that on my first attempt I had returned from within a day's journey of him, and that if I had then succeeded in finding him, I should have secured the whole of the valuable hunts of him and his people, which were now in possession of the Iroquois traders. On my return to the post I communicated my sentiments freely to Mr. S. in writing, regarding the oversight that had led to consequences so injurious to the Company, and went afterwards, at his own request, to talk over the matter with him. It was now decided that I should go with a party of men to establish a post against them, *i.e.* to shut the stable-door after the steed was stolen. To accomplish this object supplies of every kind must be hauled on sledges by the men, at an enormous expense, and after all we could not furnish the means of competing with the Iroquois with any prospect of advantage. I however lost no time in executing the orders of my superior, and set off with as many men as could be spared for the purpose.

On arriving at our destination, we built a temporary hut for our own accommodation, and a small store for the goods; but I soon discovered that the Iroquois had not only already secured all the Indians' furs, but had so completely ingratiated themselves with them that we were scarcely noticed. I remained two months in this wretched situation, and, as Mr. S.'s instructions left me in some measure to the exercise of my own judgment, I resolved on transferring the *honourable* charge to persons less sanguine than myself, and returned to my post, where I knew my services could be turned to better account. In returning I happened to fall in with a small band of Indians, who had not yet been visited by the Iroquois, one of whom was the brother of the Algonquin chief, who had been so severely chastised the preceding winter. At his lodge I passed the night, and was not only treated with the usual Indian hospitality, but received a very pressing invitation to return with a supply of goods, which he promised to trade.

Such invitations are never neglected. The moment I arrived at my post I laid aside the articles required by the Indians, and after one day's rest, started, myself and two men, carrying everything on our backs. It being late in the season, we encountered every possible difficulty on our way: the small streams overflowed, and the ice was so bad on the rivers as to preclude travelling on them. We were therefore under the necessity of taking to the woods, through a horridly rugged country, now ascending hills so steep that we could only scramble up their sides by holding on by the branches and underwood, the descent on the opposite side being equally difficult and laborious; now forcing our way through deep ravines overgrown with underwood, all but impervious; sinking to the ground at every step, and raising on our snow-shoes a load of half-melted snow, which strained the tendons of the legs and caused acute pain.

Early in the morning of the sixth day we arrived at the camp, but, to our astonishment, neither heard the voice nor saw the form of a human being, though there were infallible signs that the camp was inhabited. It was the sugar season. I entered the great man's hut with a cautious step, and found every soul in it fast asleep. I marked with surprise the confusion that prevailed around,—sugar kettles upset, pots, pans, wearing apparel, blankets, and other articles, scattered about in every direction;—what could it mean? I awoke the chief, and the mystery was solved. He appeared to be just recovering from the effects of the night's debauch,—the Iroquois were in the camp. Mine host "grinned horribly a ghastly smile" as he placed himself, rather unsteadily, in a sitting posture in his bed, and in a hoarse tremulous voice bade me welcome, at the same time rousing his better-half, who appeared to be in the same *happy* state as himself.

A clatter ensued that soon set the whole household in motion, and I hastened to make the customary offering of a small keg of rum to the chief, and another of shrub to the squaw, who immediately ordered a young woman (the family drudge) to prepare my breakfast. Meanwhile the chief, along with two of his relatives, amused himself quaffing his nectar, which evidently began to have its usual effects, and from the expressions I overheard, I could gather that he had neither forgotten his brother's treatment last winter, nor forgiven me the part I had acted on the occasion. I listened with affected indifference for a time to the taunts he began to throw out, and at last, to get rid of them, went to visit the other huts, where I found the Iroquois preparing for their departure; they had several parcels of beaver, which they took no pains to conceal from me, but there was still much more remaining.

After seeing them depart I returned to my chief, who received me with a volley of abuse, in which he was joined by his associates. The women, who were sober, observing by my looks that I was getting excited, requested me to withdraw. I did so, but was followed by the chief to the next hut, which I quitted immediately; I found myself still pursued by the same insufferable insolence. My philosophy being unequal to so severe a trial, I turned upon my tormentor, and seizing him by the throat, dashed him to the ground, and left him there speechless. I then made for a hut a short distance apart from the others, belonging to a *tête de boule,* where I remained in quietness for about the space of fifteen minutes; when suddenly my Canadian came rushing into the hut, his countenance betraying the utmost alarm, and staring me wildly in the face, he stammered out, "Les sauvages! les sauvages, monsieur, prennent leurs armes! Sauvons-nous! Sauvons-nous!" The Iroquois, coming in the next instant, confirmed his report; but I had, in fact, been flying the whole morning, and thought it now high time to take my stand. My Iroquois appearing quite calm, I told him I was determined not to stir from the spot, and asked if he would remain with me.

"I came here for that purpose," said he, "and shall stand by you to the last."

Our *tête de boule* had two guns, which he loaded; Sabourin had his, which he promised to use in his own defence: thus prepared, we awaited the expected attack. The remainder of the day, however, passed without molestation, and after night-fall, I sent out my trusty Iroquois to reconnoitre; he soon returned with the welcome intelligence that the Indians had all retired to rest. We did the same.

Next morning I went to the chief's lodge, and found him perfectly sober; I saluted him according to custom, which he returned with a scowl, repeating my words in a contemptuous manner; this exasperated my yet excited feelings to the highest degree. I felt assured that the fellow had invited me on purpose to insult me, if not for a worse purpose; and, addressing him in language that plainly bespoke my feelings, I immediately ordered my men to prepare for our departure. He remained silent for a moment, and then whispered in his wife's ear; she turned round to me, smiling, and asked if I had not brought the goods, my men were packing up, to trade?

"Yes," I replied.

"Then," said she, "you must not be in such a hurry to go away."

The husband now spoke to me in a conciliatory tone, begging me to place all that had happened to the account of the "fire-water," and for heaven's sake not to acquaint his father with his conduct.

This I readily assented to; we entered upon business, and nearly all the goods I had were exchanged for their full value in beaver. We found the travelling much better on our return, the small streams having subsided, and the snow so much diminished, that we could walk without snow-shoes.

> **Footnote 9:** "Derouine,"—a trading visit to the Indians.
>
> **Footnote 10:** When Indians remove in winter, in passing on rivers and lakes, they stick, at intervals, in the snow, branches of balsam, inclining in the direction they may have gone. In the woods, small saplings are cut or broken down; if there is no underwood, an occasional "blaze" serves as a sign-post to the experienced woodsman.
>
> **Footnote 11:** "Brulé," a part of the forest consumed by fire.

CHAPTER XI

The Iroquois passed early in spring with eighteen Indian packs in their canoes,—each pack might be estimated at 60*l.*,—our other opponent started for Montreal about the same time as last year, and I was ordered down to Fort Coulonge to take Mr. S.'s place for the summer. He returned from Montreal about the end of August, and I was much gratified to learn from him that I had been again appointed to the charge of the Chats, so that all the merit or demerit of good or bad management would now be entirely my own. A few days after, a middle-sized canoe arrived, manned by three Canadians, with whom I embarked for the scene of my first essay as an Indian trader.

On arriving at the post, I was surprised to find an old Canadian and his *cara sposa* in possession,—a circumstance of which I had had no previous intimation. This worthy pair seemed determined to maintain their position in defiance of me; and not wishing to employ violent means to dispossess them if it could possibly be done otherwise, I passed the night in the hall. Having, however, obtained possession of the outworks, I was determined to carry the citadel; and, summoning the contumacious occupants into my presence next morning, I demanded, in a peremptory tone, the immediate surrender of the keys.

"Show me your authority," said he.

"If I do not show it, you shall feel it presently!"

Seeing that I ordered my men to put my threat into execution, Jean Baptiste assumed a more humble attitude, and requested me, as a favour, to permit him to remain in the kitchen until he could find a passage to Montreal;—with this request I willingly complied.

My old opponent had still a post in this district, and I was directed to send a party in opposition to him; which being done, I remained quiet until the winter communication became practicable, when I determined on paying a visit to my friends in the Fort Coulonge district. The distance being short, and my object having no connexion with the Company's interests, I set off on my pleasure jaunt alone. I put up the first night at a sort of tavern just then opened by an American at the upper end of the Chats' Lake, the only habitation at that time in the quarter, whence I started at early dawn, expecting to reach Fort Coulonge before night. The lumbermen having commenced sledging their winter supplies, the road formed by these vehicles presented a hard, smooth surface, on which I made good speed, as I had nothing to encumber me, save my blanket and tomahawk.

Arriving at a long bend of the river about 2 P.M., I put on my snow-shoes to cut across the point and meet the road again, flattering myself that I should thus shorten the distance some two or three miles. The weather being mild, and the sun overcast, I was as much at a loss to find my way in the woods as if I had been blindfolded; I nevertheless continued my onward course, and again came on the road. I proceeded in high spirits for a considerable time, when I perceived a man before me going in the same direction with myself; quickening my pace I soon came up with him, and asked him if he was bound for the Fort?

"I guess I don't know of any fort in this part of the world," said he.

"What! not know of Fort Coulonge, and you so near to it? are you not going there?"

"I have heard of such a place," said Jonathan; "but I'd take a tarnation long time to get to it, I calculate, if I followed my nose as it points now."

I told him who I was, whither bound, and where I slept last night.

"I guess then you had better sleep there again, for it is not quite three miles off."

This was the result of making a short cut, and I resolved to follow the long and sure road in future.

A shanty that had been recently occupied, afforded me comfortable lodgings for the night, and I arrived at Fort Coulonge about noon next day, where I passed the night, and started for the outpost. Here I remained two days, and would have remained still longer, had it not been discovered one morning that our opponents were off in the direction of my outpost on the Bonne Chere. As the Indians in that quarter were excellent hunters, and owed me much, I deemed it advisable to follow them; my friends, too, sent an interpreter and three men along with me, for the purpose of trading what they could on account of their own post—*chacun pour soi* being the order of the day.

We soon overtook our opponents, and I resolved, if possible, to give them the slip by the way. Accordingly, when within a day's journey of the establishment, I pretended to have sprained my foot so badly, that I walked with the greatest seeming difficulty. My men, who were aware of the ruse, requested me to place my bundle on their sledges, to enable me to keep up with them. This farce commenced in the evening. Next morning my leg was worse than ever, until we came on the river at about ten miles' distance from the post. I was delighted to find but little snow upon the ice, so that I had a fair opportunity of putting the metal of my legs to the test, and the opposition party having sledges heavily laden, I walked hard, my foot on a sudden becoming perfectly sound, in order to tire them as much as possible before I bolted. Having apparently effected my purpose, I set off at the top of my speed, and never looked behind me until I had cleared the first long reach, when turning round, I saw a man in pursuit about half-way across; I started again, and saw no more of my pursuer.

On arriving at the post I was gratified to learn that the Indians, whom I was so anxious about, had been in a few days previously, while our opponents were off in another direction; so that they had been seen by none save our own people. Finding two men at home, I proceeded with them to the Indian camp, and arrived at dawn of day. I met with a very friendly reception, and had the good fortune to prevail upon the Indians to deliver me their furs upon the spot, which formed a very heavy load for both myself and men. We met our opponents in returning; but though they had ocular proof of my success, they nevertheless went on to the camp.

Having arrived at the post, I found some Indians there all intoxicated; I was also mortified to find the person in charge in the same state. I immediately displaced him, and made over the charge, *pro tempore*, to one of the men. The conduct of my worthless deputy hurt me so much that I could not remain another night under the same roof with him. I therefore set off on my return to the Chats, although already late in the afternoon, expecting to reach the first shanty in the early part of the night.

The Bonne Chere river is very rapid in the upper part, and does not "set fast"12 until late in the season, unless the cold be very intense. I arrived at this part soon after night-fall, and perceiving by the clear light of the moon the dangers in my way, I deemed it imprudent to proceed farther; and having nothing to strike fire with, I cut a few branches of balsam and strewed them under the spreading boughs of a large cedar, and wrapping myself up in my blanket, lay down. The weather being mild, I thought I could sleep comfortably without fire; but was mistaken. When I awoke from my first sleep, which must have been sound, I found my limbs stiff with cold, while my teeth chattered violently in my head. To remain in this condition till daylight was almost certain death; I resolved, therefore, at all hazards to find my way to the shanty, which might be about ten miles distant. The light of the moon being very bright, enabled me to avoid the openings in the ice, and by moving on cautiously, about three o'clock in the morning I reached the shanty; which belonged to a warm-hearted son of Erin, who received me with the characteristic hospitality of his countrymen, placing before me the best his cabin afforded, and with his own blankets and those of his men making up a comfortable bed, on which I slept till late in the day, and next night in my own bed.

As the greater part of my customers wintered in the vicinity of the outpost, and I had no longer any confidence in the person in charge there, I resolved on passing the remainder of the winter at it myself; I therefore requested that a person should be sent up from the Lake of Two Mountains to take care of the establishment during my absence. On the arrival of this person, I proceeded to the outpost, but shall pass over the transactions that occurred there, being similar in all respects to those already narrated. One circumstance, however, occurred, which, though not in my vocation, I think worthy of notice.

Two itinerant missionaries called at the Lake of Two Mountains and distributed a number of religious tracts among the natives, together with a few copies of the Gospel according to St. John, in the Indian language. My Algonquin interpreter happened to get one of the latter, and took much pleasure in reading it. Towards the latter end of the season I received a packet from my superior at the Lake, and, to my surprise, found in it a letter with the seal of the Church affixed, addressed to my interpreter, which I put into his hands, and observed him perusing very attentively. Soon after he called me aside, and told me that the letter in question conveyed a peremptory command from the priest to destroy the bad book he had in his possession, or else his child that died in autumn would be denied the rites of Christian sepulture.

We are told that the age of bigotry is past: facts like this prove the contrary. I asked him if he intended to obey the commands of his ghostly father. "Not exactly," said he; "I shall send the book to him, and let him do with it what he pleases; for my part, I have read it over and over again, and find it all good, very good; why the 'black coat' should call it bad is a mystery to me."

Footnote 12: Freeze.

CHAPTER XII

Early in spring I returned to the Chats, and after the close of the trade took my departure for Montreal, having finished my apprenticeship. I renewed my contract for three years, and was appointed to the charge of Lac de Sable, a post situated on a tributary of the Ottawa, called *Rivière aux Lièvres*, two hundred miles distant from Montreal.

I embarked on the 15th August, 1826, and arrived at the post on the 1st September; where I was gratified to find a comfortable dwelling-house, and a large farm with pigs, poultry, and cattle in abundance. All this was very well, but there was also a powerful opposition, and I had experience enough to know that the enjoyment of any kind of comfort is incompatible with the life we lead in opposition.

The difficulties of my situation, moreover, were from various causes extremely perplexing. The old North-West agents, acting for the Hudson's Bay Company in Canada, had declared a bankruptcy the preceding winter; the principal manager having quitted the country rather precipitately, as was supposed, and forgotten to appoint a successor; the management devolved in consequence upon the head accountant, Mr. C— —e, who, however well he might be qualified for the duties of the situation, felt the responsibility of acting without authority to be too great, and confined himself accordingly to such measures only as he was confident would subject him to no inconvenience when the day of reckoning arrived. Meantime the business of this department sustained a serious check; the old hands of the post, having been tampered with by the opposition in the course of last winter, quitted the service to a man, and I now found the establishment to consist of a clerk, interpreter, and one man only. I was given to understand that three men additional would join me as soon as they could, and that I must not expect any more; thus our number would be seven against twenty-two.

A disparity so vast precluded all hopes of maintaining the contest with advantage to the Company or credit to myself. Fortune, however, declared in our favour; dissensions arose in the ranks of our opponents, clerks and men deserted, supplies for trade ran short, and from being the weaker party we were now the stronger.

Governor Simpson having taken up his residence at La Chine in autumn, men and goods were furnished in abundance, and the petty traders were made to see, ere the winter passed, the futility of entering the lists in competition with a Company possessing so vast resources.

Mr. MacD— —l having wintered two years at this post, and being consequently well acquainted with the natives, I entrusted the direction of affairs against the opposition entirely to him, and remained quietly at home, having only the few Indians that wintered in the neighbourhood of the post to attend to; my situation, however, was often far from agreeable, being frequently reduced to the company of my pigs and poultry for weeks together, and obliged to act as trader, cook, hewer of wood, and drawer of water.

In the course of the winter I was favoured with a visit from Mr. F— —r, to whose district this post had just been annexed, and had the gratification to receive, through him, a letter from Governor Simpson, conveying, in very flattering terms, his approbation of my conduct. I was told that I was in the direct road to preferment—that my merits should be represented to the Council on his arrival in the interior—and that he should be happy to have an opportunity of recommending me to the Governor and Committee, when he returned to England. We shall see, in the sequel, how these promises were fulfilled.

I embarked, on the 15th June, 1827, for Montreal, and found Mr. K— —h, a chief factor in the service, at the head of affairs; and my outfit being prepared in a few days, I re-embarked, taking my passage, as formerly, on board of a large canoe, deeply laden. The last rapid and portage on the Rivière aux Lièvres is within eight miles of the establishment, and generally takes the men a day to pass it. Arriving at this place late in the evening, I resolved on going on a-foot; it being fine moonlight, I felt confident of finding my way without difficulty. The weather having been immoderately hot for some time past, I had sat in the canoe divested of my upper garments, and thought I might, without inconvenience, dispense with them now, as I expected to reach the house ere the night air could prove injurious to me.

Setting off, therefore, in "light marching order," I immediately gained the high grounds, in order to keep clear of the underwood that covers the banks of the river; and just as the moon appeared above the surrounding hills, arrived on the banks of a small stream, where I observed a portage path sunk deep in the ground, a circumstance which proved it to be much frequented—by whom or for what purpose I could not say, for I had seldom passed the limits of my farm during last winter, and was nearly as ignorant of the topography of the environs as the first day I arrived. I had not heard of the existence of a river in the quarter, nor did I imagine there was any; the conclusion I arrived at therefore was, that I had lost my way, and that my most eligible course was, to endeavour to find the main stream, and by following it, retrace my course to the portage.

I soon fell on the river, but my retrograde march proved exceedingly toilsome; at every step I was obliged to bend the branches of the underwood to one side and another, or pressing them down under my feet, force my way through by main strength: some short spaces indeed intervened, that admitted of an easier passage; still my progress was so slow that the sun appeared before I reached the upper end of the portage. Finding an old canoe here, belonging to the post, I resolved on crossing to the opposite side of the river, where I knew there was a path that led to the house, by which the Indians often passed when travelling in small canoes. I accordingly ran to the lower end of the portage for a paddle, where I found my men still asleep; and having heard that the lower end of this path came out exactly opposite to the upper end of the portage, I struck out into the woods the moment I landed, fancying that I could not fail to discover it.

The sun got higher and higher as I proceeded, and I went faster and yet faster, to no purpose;—no path appeared; and I at length became convinced that I was lost—being equally in difficulty to find my way back to the river as forward to the post.

The weather was very sultry; and such had been the drought of the season that all the small creeks were dried up, so that I could nowhere procure a drop of water to moisten my parched lips. The sensations occasioned by thirst are so much more painful than those we feel from hunger, that although I had eaten but little the preceding day, and nothing on that day, I never thought of food. While my inner man was thus tortured by thirst, my outer man scarcely suffered less from another cause. The country through which I passed being of a marshy nature, I was incessantly tormented by the venomous flies that abound in such situations,—my shirt, and only other habiliment, having sustained so much damage in my nocturnal expedition, that the insects had free access *partout*.13

I came to the foot of a high hill about two o'clock P.M., which I ascended, and got a very good view of the surrounding country from its summit; hills and lakes appeared in every direction; but the sight of these objects only served to impress my mind with the conviction, that, unless Providence should direct my steps to the establishment, the game was up with me. Having descended, I sauntered about the remainder of the day, my ideas becoming more and more bewildered, and my strength declining; and passed the night sometimes sitting, sometimes standing, sometimes moving about;—but sitting, standing, or moving about, subjected to the same tortures.

I endeavoured during the night to compose my mind as much as possible; some happy thought might perchance suggest itself, which might lead to my deliverance. Nor were my efforts without some success: I called to mind the position of the post with respect to the rising and setting sun; another circumstance of importance also recurred to me.

A Canadian hunter, who received his supplies at my post, had told me that such Indians as did not wish to pay their debts at the post, frequently passed unperceived by a chain of small lakes that ran parallel to the river, and extended from Lac de Sable to somewhere near the rapid, whence I had taken my departure. I recollected, too, his having mentioned that some Indian families occasionally made sugar on the borders of these lakes, and that a good path lay from their camp to the post. Having passed the night in a deep valley, the sun did not appear until late in the morning, when I shaped my course, to the best of my judgment, for the post. Two or three hours' walk brought me to the foot of a high hill, nearly destitute of wood on one side; and expecting that some discovery might be made from the top which might be of use to me, I resolved on attempting the ascent—an undertaking of no small difficulty in my enfeebled state. I succeeded in gaining the top, and to my unspeakable joy, perceived a chain of lakes within about two miles of me, exactly corresponding to the description given me by the Canadian hunter. I also heard the reports of guns, but so indistinctly that I could not determine the direction the report came from. Noting with the utmost care the course that would lead me to the lakes, I descended the steep declivity with a degree of speed that surprised myself,—such is the powerful influence the mind exercises over the body.

I expected an hour's walk would bring me to the lakes, but the sun being in the zenith, and my way lying through a dense forest of pine, I could not keep a straight course. I proceeded onward, however, as well as *reason* could direct me, and most willingly would I have exchanged a little of that *faculty* for the *instinct* that leads the brute creation with unerring certainty through the pathless depths of the forest.

The sun was rapidly declining, and my hopes with it, when suddenly I fancied I heard the murmuring sound of running water. Could it be really so? What a delightful feast I should have! for I had passed the day, like the preceding, without a drop of water to allay my raging thirst. I listened; the sound became more distinct—it was no illusion. I quickened my pace, and soon came upon a charming rivulet, flowing rapidly over a bed of white pebbles, its water clear as crystal. I rushed into the midst of it, and fervently thanking the Giver of all good, threw myself on my knees, and drank draught after draught till my thirst was quenched. I felt refreshed to an extraordinary degree, and concluding that the stream would lead me to the river, or to some lake communicating with it, I followed its course, wading in the water that there might be "no mistake," and soon came out on the border of a small lake, where I had the additional satisfaction of hearing the report of guns so distinctly as to convince me that the party firing them could be at no great distance. I walked round the lake, and at its far end fell on a portage path that soon conducted me to another lake. This, then, must be the chain of lakes I was in search of! I was transported at the thought.

But an incident soon occurred that served to damp at once my spirits and my person: a distant peal of thunder was heard; peal after peal succeeded; the heavens were obscured, and heavy drops of rain, the harbingers of an approaching storm, fell from the dark clouds. I strained every nerve to reach the firing party ere the storm should burst upon me. I reached the foot of the hill, but the firing had ceased. I nevertheless ascended as quickly as my wearied limbs would carry me, but on reaching the spot found no one there.

The storm now burst upon me in all its fury. Flash followed flash in quick succession, and the rain fell in torrents, which, however, as the few clothes that still adhered to my person were already saturated by the previous rain, caused me but little additional inconvenience. I descended to the lake, and by the time I reached the far end of it the darkness had increased so much, that I could proceed no farther. Perceiving an old encampment—a few half-decayed branches of balsam, at the foot of a large hemlock—I took up my quarters there for the night. The tufted branches of this tree render it a much more secure retreat in a thunder-storm than the pine, whose pointed branches and spiral shaped top frequently attract the electric fluid.

Towards morning the storm seemed to have expended its fury; and, strange to say, in the midst of it I enjoyed two or three hours' sleep. Nature had been so exhausted by protracted sufferings, that (though the flies were driven to their covert) I believe I could have slept upon a bed of thorns, covered with gnats and mosquitoes. As soon as it was sufficiently clear to enable me to find my way, I quitted my hemlock and fell on the portage path, which soon led me to another small lake, and which I proceeded to circumambulate as usual, keeping a sharp look-out for the path that led to the post; when suddenly the report of a gun burst from an adjoining hill. At the same instant, I observed a net pole standing in the water at the bottom of a small bay close by, and directed my steps towards it; when on approaching it I discovered a broad path ascending from the water's edge, and immediately after the buildings of a sugar camp.

Allowing the party on the hill to blaze away, I followed the path, and in less than half-an-hour came out upon the Rivière aux Lièvres, immediately opposite the house. I perceived the men of the establishment, with some

Indians, all in a bustle; some preparing to embark in a canoe, others firing. I sat down to gaze for a moment on the most interesting scene I had ever witnessed, and then gave a loud cry, which it was evident nobody heard, although the river is not more than a stone-cast across. I made a second effort with better success. The Indians raised a shout of triumph; the men hallooed,

"Le voilà! le voilà! Je le vois! Je le vois à l'autre bord! Embarquez! embarquez!"

A few minutes more, and I found myself restored to at best a prolonged life of misery and exile. Let it not be inferred from this expression that I felt ungrateful for my deliverance; on the contrary, my escape from a death so lingering and terrible made a deep impression upon my mind. I afterwards gave a holiday to my men in remembrance of it, and made them all happy for one day.

> **Footnote 13:** There are three different kinds of these tormenting insects, viz. the mosquito, the black-fly, and the gnat—the latter the same as the midge in N. Britain—who relieve each other regularly in the work of torture. The mosquitoes continue at their post from dawn to eight or nine o'clock, A.M.; the black-flies succeed, and remain in the field till near sunset; the mosquitoes again mount guard till dark, and are finally succeeded by the gnats, who continue their watch and incessant attacks till near sunrise.

CHAPTER XIII

Nothing occurred this year out of the usual routine, save an accident that happened to myself, and had nearly proved fatal. A couple of hounds had been presented to me by a friend, for the purpose of hunting the deer that abounded in the neighbourhood. The dogs having one day broken loose from the leash, betook themselves to the hills; and the first intimation we had of their being at liberty, was the sound of their voices in full cry on an adjacent hill. I instantly seized my gun, and following a beaten track that led to a small lake at the base of the hill, I perceived a deer swimming towards an island in the middle of the lake, and only a little beyond the range of gun-shot. An old fishing-canoe happening to be at hand, I immediately launched it, and gave chase, without examining the condition it was in. I proceeded but a short distance, however, when I perceived that it leaked very much. I continued, nevertheless, to paddle, till I got nearly half-way across to the island; but by this time the quantity of water in the canoe had increased so much, that my ardour for the chase began to give way to anxiety for my own safety. I perceived a large hole in the stern of the canoe, now almost level with the surface of the lake, through which the water gushed with every stroke of the paddle. The fore-part appearing free from injury, I immediately inverted my position,—a movement necessarily effected with much difficulty in so small a craft; and having thus placed myself, the stern was consequently raised a little higher. I then paddled gently towards a long point projecting from the mainland, much nearer me than the island; and although I used the utmost caution in paddling, the canoe sunk under me some distance from the shore. The lake, however, was fortunately shallow at this place, so that I soon found bottom. Had there been the least ripple on the water, I could not have escaped; but the weather was perfectly calm, and the lake smooth as glass.

In the early part of next winter, I went again in pursuit of the deer; and although I incurred no great risk of losing my life, I yet experienced such inconveniences as seldom fall to the lot of amateur hunters in other parts of the world. I left the house early in the morning, and, starting a deer close by, gave chase, following the track over hill and dale, until I reached a high ridge bordering on Lac de Sable. Here the deer slackened his pace, and appeared, by his track, to have descended slowly into a valley, where he remained until I started him a second time. I still continued the pursuit, without thinking of time or distance from the establishment. At length the night evidently began to close, and I felt faint and exhausted from want of food, and the exertions I had made during the day. I therefore gave up the chase; but to retrace my steps by the devious path by which I had pursued the deer, would have occupied the greater part of the night; I therefore resolved on returning by a more direct course; but the upshot was, that, after wandering about for some time, and repeatedly falling on my own tracks, I passed the night in the woods. Although nearly overcome with fatigue, I durst not think of lying down, well knowing what the consequence would be; I therefore walked backwards and forwards, on a beaten track, the whole night; and next morning adopted the sure course of finding my way by my tracks of the preceding day. Meeting an Indian by the way, who had been sent in search of me, he led me by a short cut, and we arrived at the house about two o'clock, P.M.

In the autumn of 1829, another opponent entered the lists against us,— an enterprising Canadian, who had been for a long time in the Company's service. This adventurer proceeded some distance inland, and I need scarcely say that a party was sent to keep him company. Understanding that the new competitor gave our people more trouble than had been anticipated, I determined on taking an active part in the game; and as I had only two men with me at Lac de Sable, whose services were required there, I set off alone, intending to take with me an Indian who had an encampment by the way, as I was unacquainted with the route. I slept at the Indian's wigwam, who readily accompanied me next morning; but the weather being intolerably cold, the poor fellow got both his ears frozen, *et aliud quidquam præterea*, in crossing a large lake not far from his camp. The moment he perceived his mishap, he assailed me in the most abusive terms, and swore that he would accompany me no farther; which, being conscious that I was partly the cause of his misfortune, I bore with as much equanimity as I could; and arriving at the opposite side of the lake, we kindled a fire, and I proceeded to treat his case according to the usual practice; that is, rubbing the part affected with snow, or bathing it with cold water until it is thawed, and the circulation restored. Having happily succeeded, I forthwith dismissed him, and determined to find my way alone; and having a tolerable idea of the direction in which I should go, and the weather being clear, I entertained no doubt of falling somewhere on the river whereon the post is situated. I came upon it, as it seemed to me, a considerable distance below the establishment, just as the sun was setting.

Having travelled in deep snow the whole day, I felt so much fatigued that I could scarcely exert myself sufficiently to keep my body warm, the cold being intense. I walked as briskly as my diminished strength would allow; but at length became so weak, that I was obliged to lay myself down at short intervals. In this wretched state,—my limbs benumbed with cold, and thinking I should never see daylight,—I suddenly came upon a hard beaten path: this inspired me with new vigour, as it indicated the close vicinity of a shanty. I soon discovered the desired haven, and crawling up the steep bank that led to it, I knocked at the door with my snow-shoes, and was immediately admitted.

The noise I made roused the inmates, who had been sound asleep; and who, seeing my helpless condition, exerted themselves in every possible way to relieve me. I was nearly in the last stage of exhaustion, being unable to take off my snow-shoes, or even articulate a word. One of these noble woodsmen guided me next day to the post; when, as a small mark of gratitude for his generous kindness, I presented him and his companions with what is always acceptable to a shanty-man, a liberal allowance of the "crathur," to enjoy themselves withal.

If it be asked why I did not make a fire, when I had the necessary apparatus; I answer, that I had but a very small axe, quite unfit for felling so large timber as grew on the banks of this river; and I was, besides, so benumbed and exhausted as to be unequal to the task even of lighting a fire.

Sometime after my return from Montreal in the autumn of 1830, I went to pay a visit to one of my customers whose lands were at a considerable distance. I was accompanied by one man in a small canoe; and as it was necessary that one of us should carry the canoe over the portages, and the other the property, I chose the former, being the lightest though by far the most inconvenient load. I found it very oppressive at first, but use rendered it more easy. This was the first time I carried a canoe.

On our return from the Indian's camp we met with rather a disagreeable accident, while ascending a small and very rapid river. In pushing forward the canoe against the stream, my pole happened to glance off a stone, and the canoe swinging round came in contact with the trunk of a tree projecting from the bank, and we, or at least I, was upset in an instant. Fortunately the current, though strong, was smooth and free from whirlpools; so that, after swimming down a short distance in search of a landing-place, I rejoined my companion, whom I found standing on the bank perfectly dry. On inquiring of him how he happened to avoid a ducking, he told me he sprang ashore while I was attempting to parry off the tree; doubtless his having done so was in a great measure the cause of the accident. He, however, acted a very prudent part after landing, having caught hold of the canoe in the act of upsetting, and thus preserved the goods from being lost or damaged.

In the course of this year, the Iroquois and Algonquins were nearly coming to blows on account of the hunting-grounds. This quarrel originated from a speech which Colonel McKay, then at the head of the Indian department, had addressed to the Iroquois, in which, making use of the metaphorical language of the people, he observed that Indians of all tribes ought to live together in the utmost concord and amity, seeing they inhabited the same villages, "and ate out of the same dish." This the Iroquois interpreted in a way more suitable to their own wishes than consistent with its real meaning. "Our father," said they, "tells us we eat out of the same dish with the Algonquins;—he means that we have an equal right to the hunting-grounds." They proceeded, accordingly, to avail themselves of the supposed privilege. The consequence was a very violent quarrel, in which Government was ultimately obliged to interfere.

The Indians informed us, this spring, of a dreadful murder that had been committed in the early part of the winter by some of the natives of Hudson's Bay. The particulars of this tale of blood I since learned from an individual that escaped from the massacre. The Indians attached to the posts established along the shores of Hudson's Bay are comparatively civilized; most of them speak English, and are employed as voyageurs by the Company. Few or no precautions are taken at these posts to guard against treachery; the gates are seldom shut, and some of the posts are destitute of palisades or defence of any kind. Of this description was the post where the catastrophe occurred which I am about to relate.

The post of Hannah Bay is situated about sixty miles to the north of Moose Factory, and was at this time under the charge of a Mr. Corrigal. His establishment consisted of two or three half-breeds, and an Indian who had been brought up by the whites. He and some of the men had families. In the course of the winter five Indians came in with their "hunts," and agreeably to their usual practice encamped close by. Those Indians are designated "Home Guards,"—a term generally applied to the Indians attached to a trading post; they hunt in winter at a convenient distance from the post, and are employed in summer as voyageurs, or in performing any other necessary duty. Notwithstanding their thus being frequently in company with white men and Christians, they still retain many of the barbarous habits, and much of the superstitious belief of their forefathers, aggravated, I regret to say, by some of the vices of the whites.

Among the number of those just mentioned was an individual who had acquired considerable influence among his tribe, from his pretending to be skilled in the art of divination. This man told his fellows that he had had a communication from the Great Spirit, who assured him that he would become the greatest man in Hudson's Bay if he only followed the course prescribed to him, which was, first, to cut off their own trading post, and then with the spoil got there to hire other Indians, who should assist in destroying all the other posts the Company possessed in the country. Accordingly, it was determined to carry their design into execution, whenever a favourable opportunity occurred. This was not long in presenting itself. They came one day to the establishment, and told the people that the "man of medicine" had come for the purpose of performing some extraordinary feat that would astonish them all. The silly creatures believed the story, and went to the borders of the lake, where they observed the sorcerer showing off a variety of antics very much to their amusement. The conspirators, seeing this part of the stratagem succeed, rushed into the house, and immediately despatched Mr. Corrigal and his family. The men, hearing the report of the guns, hastened back towards the house. The two that first arrived were saluted by a volley of balls; the one fell dead, the other fled. The third, seeing what had happened, seized his youngest child, and also fled. The murderers pursued. The poor fellow, encumbered by the weight of his child, necessarily fell behind. A ball from the pursuers killed the child, and wounded him in the hand. Dropping, then, the lifeless body, he soon came up with his fellow, and both escaped without further injury.

It was about noon when they began their flight. One of them reached Moose Factory next day about noon, the other soon after. The distance—nearly sixty miles—travelled in so short a space of time, may appear incredible; but fear gave them wings, they fled for their lives and never halted. One of them, my informant, lost all the toes of one of his feet by the frost.

Measures were immediately adopted to frustrate the further diabolical designs of the Indians, as well as to avenge the innocent blood that had been shed. Messengers were despatched with all possible haste to Rupert's house, the nearest post, to give the alarm, and a party of men, under an efficient leader, was sent to seize the murderers. This expedition, however, proved unsuccessful, as the Indians could not be found in that direction; but, in the meantime, two of them who had come to Rupert's house to "spy the land," were seized and sent bound to Moose Factory, and one of them was compelled to act as guide to another party. Led by him, they approached the camp without being perceived, and found the "man of medicine" sitting very composedly in his tent, surrounded by the spoils he had taken from the fort. He was secured, and the rest of his associates, who were absent hunting, were soon "tracked," and secured likewise. They then all underwent the punishment they deserved.

The fort presented a horrible spectacle. Men, women, and children shared the same fate, and the mangled limbs of their victims were scattered among the articles of property which the wretches, not being able to carry off with them, had attempted to destroy.

CHAPTER XIV

Finding that my presence was more wanted at the outpost than elsewhere, I resolved on taking up my residence there for the winter 1831-32. Our active opponent gave us much annoyance, causing great expense to the Company, without any benefit to himself; on the contrary, it ultimately ruined him.

While accompanying our party on a trading excursion in the beginning of winter, I had a very narrow escape. We were travelling on the Gatineau, a very rapid stream that joins the Ottawa, a little below Hull. A young lad, interpreter to the opposition, and I, had one morning gone considerably in advance of the others, walking smartly to keep ourselves warm, when I suddenly broke through the ice. The current here running strong, I should soon have been swept under the ice, had I not, by extending my arms upon it on either side of me, kept my head above water. At the hazard of his own life, my companion came to my assistance; but the ice was too weak to admit of his approaching sufficiently near to reach me his hand; he therefore cut a long pole, and tying his belt to it, threw it to me; and laying hold of it, I dragged myself on the sound ice. But the danger was not yet over; the weather was intensely cold, so that my clothes were soon frozen solid upon me, and having no means of lighting a fire, I ran into the woods; and in order to keep my body from being frozen into the same mass with my clothes, continued running up and down with all my might, till the rest of the party arrived.

I had a still more narrow escape in the month of March ensuing. I had been on a visit to the post under my own immediate charge, termed head-quarters *par excellence*; returning to the post alone, I came to a place where our men, in order to avoid a long detour occasioned by a high and steep hill coming close to the river, were accustomed to draw their sledges upon the ice along the edge of a rapid. About the middle of the rapid, where the torrent is fiercest, the banks of the river are formed of rocks rising almost perpendicularly from the water's edge; and here they had to pass on a narrow ledge of ice, between the rock on the one side, and the foaming and boiling surge on the other. The ledge, at no time very broad, was now reduced, by the falling in of the water, to a strip of ice of about eighteen inches, or little more, adhering to the rock. The ice, however, seemed perfectly solid, and I made no doubt that, with caution, I should succeed in passing safely this formidable strait.

The weather having been very mild in the fore-part of the day, my shoes and socks had been saturated with wet, but were now frozen hard by the cold of the approaching night. Overlooking this circumstance, I attempted the dangerous passage; and had proceeded about halfway, when my foot slipped, and I suddenly found myself resting with one hip on the border of ice, while the rest of my body overhung the rapid rushing fearfully underneath. I was now literally in a state of agonizing suspense: to regain my footing was impossible; even the attempt to move might precipitate me into the rapid.

My first thought indeed was to throw myself in, and endeavour by swimming to reach the solid ice that bridged the river a short distance below; a glance at the torrent convinced me that this was a measure too desperate to be attempted;—I should have been dashed against the ice, or hurried beneath it by the current. But my time was not yet come. Within a few feet of the spot where I was thus suspended *in sublimis*, the rock projected a little outward, so as to break the force of the current. It struck me that a new border of ice might be formed at this place, under and parallel to that on which I was perched; exploring cautiously, therefore, with a stick which I fortunately had in my hand, all along and beneath me, I found my conjecture well founded; but whether the ice were strong enough to bear me, I could not ascertain. But it was my only hope of deliverance; letting myself down therefore gently, I planted my feet on the lower ledge, and clinging with the tenacity of a shell-fish to the upper, I crept slowly along till I reached land.

This autumn, I had the satisfaction of seeing all my opponents quit the field, some of whom had maintained a long and obstinate struggle; yet, although I had reason to congratulate myself on their departure, as it promised me relief from the painfully toilsome life I had led, I must do one of the parties, at least, the justice to say, that, in different circumstances, I should have beheld their departure with regret. Dey and McGillivray carried on the contest longer than the others, and did so without showing any of that rancorous feeling which the other petty traders manifested towards the Company. MacGillivray and myself, when travelling together, often shared the same blanket, and the same kettle; and found, that while this friendly feeling was mutually advantageous to ourselves, it did not in any way compromise the interests of our employers. I parted from him, wishing him every success in *any other* line of business he might engage in.

After the removal of my competitors, I found the time to hang heavily on my hands; and the ease I had so often sighed for, I now could scarcely endure; but I was not allowed long time to sigh for a change. On the 5th of April an Iroquois came up from Montreal with a packet conveying orders to me to proceed forthwith to Lachine, whence I should embark by the opening of the navigation for the northern department. I was alone at the post when these unexpected orders came to hand, all the men being absent at the outpost; and as it behoved me to use the utmost diligence in order to get away ere winter travelling should break up, leaving an old squaw in charge, I set out for the outpost in quest of Mr. Cameron, who was appointed my successor; and on the 7th of April took my departure.

On arriving at the Grand River, I found travelling on the ice to be attended with great danger, and several accidents had already happened; but I had the good fortune to reach Grenville at the head of the Long Sault in safety; here, however, my farther progress was arrested for a fortnight, the roads being impassable. I arrived at Lachine in the end of April, and after handing in the documents relative to my late charge, Mr. K—— told me I was at liberty to spend the intervening time until the embarkation, where and how I pleased. Gratified by this indulgence, I was about to frame a speech expressive of my gratitude, when he continued,—"for, Sir, you are to understand we do not keep a boarding-house here." This stopped my mouth, and I reserved my thanks for a future occasion; for I could not but feel, that being an officer of the Company, it was robbing me of a part of my pay under the pretext of an indulgence. Availing myself, however, of this ungenerous grant of freedom, I spent some halcyon days in the company of relatives most dear to me, and expected no interruption to my enjoyment until the time appointed for the embarkation: but a few days after I had joined my relatives in the vicinity of Montreal, I received a letter, commanding me, in the most peremptory manner, to repair to Lachine,— "circumstances not foreseen at my arrival from the interior required my departure without further delay." I accompanied the bearer of Mr. K——'s letter, and found, on arriving at Lachine, that I had been appointed to conduct some of Captain Back's party, who proved rather troublesome to him at Montreal, to the Chats, and there to await my passage to the north by the Brigade.

I had now served the Hudson's Bay Company faithfully and zealously for a period of twelve years, leading a life of hardship and toil, of which no idea can be formed except by those whose hard lot it may be to know it by experience. How enthusiastically I had laboured for them, may be better gathered from the foregoing narrative than from any statement I could here make. And what was my reward? I had no sooner succeeded in freeing my district from opposition, than I was ordered to resign my situation to another, who would enjoy the fruits of my labour:—when I arrived at the Company's head-quarters to take my departure for a remote district, I was ordered to provide for myself until I embarked; and when enjoying myself in the bosom of my family, to suit the convenience of one of their correspondents, I was torn away from them prematurely, and without warning,—treatment, which caused one of them so severe a shock as nearly to prove fatal!

Before I take leave of the Montreal department, it may be well to allude more particularly to the manners and customs of the natives. The mode of life the Algonquins lead, while at their village, has been already touched upon; within these few years a great change has taken place, not in their morals, but in their circumstances. The southern and western parts of their hunting-grounds are now nearly all possessed by the white man, whose encroachments extend farther and farther every year. Beaver meadows are now to be found in place of beaver dams; and rivers are crossed on bridges formed by the hand of man, where the labours of the beaver afforded a passage for the roving Indian and hunter only a few years before.

Happy change, it may be said; but so say not the Indians; the days of happiness are gone for them, at least for those of the present generation; though I have no doubt that their posterity may, in course of time, become reconciled to, and adopt those habits of life which their altered circumstances may require. A few have done so already, but many of them still remain on the most remote parts of their lauds, having no longer the means of enjoying themselves at their village, or of satisfying the avarice of priests and traders. Here they pursue, without restraint or interruption, the mode of life most congenial to their habits.

I have already observed, that I could discover but little difference between the (so called) Christian Indians, and their unbaptized countrymen, when beyond the surveillance of their priests. They practise all the superstitious rites of their forefathers, and place implicit confidence in the power of magic, although they admit that the same results cannot be obtained now, as formerly, in consequence, as they say, "of the Cross having come in contact with the Medicine." They have their genii of lakes, rivers, mountains, and forests, to whom they offer sacrifice. I was present at the sacrifice of a beaver, made by an Algonquin to his familiar, or "totem," in order to propitiate him, because he had been unsuccessful in hunting. The beaver was roasted without being skinned, the fur only being appropriated to the spirit, whilst the flesh afforded a luxurious feast to the sacrificer; and in this part of the ceremony I willingly participated.

When any of them is taken ill, the indisposition is ascribed to the effects of "bad medicine;" and the person is mentioned whom they suspect of having laid the disease upon them. Many violent deeds are committed to revenge these supposed injuries. An Algonquin, who had lost a child, blamed a *tête de boule*, who was domiciled at Lac de Sable, for his death. The ensuing spring the *tête de boule* took a fancy to visit the Lake of Two Mountains, and set off in company with the Algonquins.

On arrival of the party at the Grand River, he who had lost his child invited the *tête de boule* to his tent, and entertained him in the most friendly manner for a time, then suddenly drawing his knife, he plunged it into the side of his unsuspecting guest. The poor wretch fled, and concealed himself in a pig-sty, where his groans soon discovered him to the Algonquin, who, again seizing him, thrust his knife into his throat, and did not withdraw it until he ceased to live.

"Now," exclaimed his murderer, "I am avenged for the death of my child. You wanted to go to the Lake to be baptized, and here I have baptized you in your own blood."

Many other instances might be adduced to prove that the savage disposition of these Indians has not been greatly ameliorated by their profession of Christianity; they have, in fact, all the vices with but few of the virtues of their heathen countrymen.

They are immoderately fond of ardent spirits, men, women and—shocking to say—children. This hateful vice, which contributes more than any other to the debasement of human nature, seems to produce more baneful effects upon the Indian, both physically and morally, than upon the European. The worst propensities of his nature are excited by it. While under the influence of this demon he spares neither friend nor foe; and in many instances the members of his own family become the victims either of his fury or his lust.

The crime of incest is by no means unknown among them; rum, the greatest scourge and curse of the Indian race, is undoubtedly the principal cause of this dreadful corruption: but is it not strange that religion should have so little effect in reforming their manners? The Mississagays, the neighbours of the Algonquins, who speak the same language, were only converted a few years ago by the Methodists, and from being the most dissipated and depraved of Indians, are now become sober, industrious and devout.

It seems, therefore, impossible even for the most unprejudiced to avoid the conclusion that the difference in manners must in a great measure be ascribed to the different methods adopted by the Roman Catholic and

Protestant missionaries in converting the natives. The Roman Catholic convert is first baptized, then instructed in the forms of worship, taught to repeat Pater nosters and Ave Marias, to make the sign of the cross, and to confess. He is now a member of the Church, and is dismissed to his woods—a Christian, can we say? The Methodists pursue a different course. Their converts must not only reform their lives, but give indubitable proofs that they are reformed; they are taught so as to understand thoroughly the sound principles of Christianity; and they must give an account of their faith, and a reason for the hope that is in them, before they are admitted as members of the Christian community. "The tree is known by its fruits."

The Sachems, or chiefs of the Algonquins, possess little or no authority, but their advice is of some weight There are gradations of rank in the chieftainship; the Kitchi Okima, or great chief, takes precedence at the Council, and propounds the subject of discussion; the inferior chiefs (Okimas) speak in turn, according to seniority; every old man, however, whether chief or not, is allowed to give his opinion, and the general voice of the assembly decides the question at issue. It is seldom, however, that any question arises requiring much deliberation in the present times of peace. When a party of strange Indians arrives at the village, a council is called to ascertain the means the community may possess of discharging properly the rites of hospitality; each individual states the modicum he is willing to contribute, in cash or in kind, and the proceeds, which are always sufficient to entertain the guests sumptuously, according to Indian ideas, while they remain, are placed at the disposal of the Kitchi Okima.

Councils are held and harangues delivered when they receive their annual presents from Government; these consist of blankets, cloth, ammunition, and a variety of small articles, all of which in their present impoverished state are highly valued by them. They profess an attachment to the British Government; but, like certain more civilized nations, they will fight for the cause that is likely to yield them most advantage. Their loyalty to Britain, therefore, is less to be depended on than their hatred to America. A general idea has gone abroad regarding their taciturnity which does not accord with my experience. Far from being averse to colloquial intercourse, they delight in it; none more welcome to an Indian wigwam than one who can talk freely. They pass the winter evenings in relating their adventures, hunting being their usual theme, or in telling stories; and often have I heard the woods resound with peals of laughter excited by their wit, for they too are witty in their own way.

Their tradition of the flood (*kitchi a tesoka*, or "great tale,") is somewhat remarkable. The world having been overflowed by water, all mankind perished but one family, who embarked in a large canoe, taking a variety of animals along with them. The canoe floated about for some time, when a musk-rat, tired of its confinement, jumped overboard and dived; it soon reappeared, with a mouthful of mud, which it deposited on the surface of the water, and from this beginning the new world was formed.

When the veracity of an Indian is doubted, he points to heaven with his forefinger, and exclaims:—

"He to whom we belong knows that what I say is true."

No white man trusts more firmly in the validity of a solemn oath than the Indian in this asseveration. Still it must be confessed that they are prone to falsehood; but they seem to allow themselves a much greater licence in this respect in their intercourse with the whites than amongst themselves.

When an Indian is about to enter a wigwam, he utters the word or sound "Quay" in a peculiar tone; the word repeated from within is considered as an invitation to enter. (Should he neglect to announce himself in this way he is considered as ill-bred—an unmannerly boor. The left-hand side of the wigwam as you enter is considered the place of honour; here the father of the family and chief squaw take their station, the young men on the opposite side, and the women next to the door, or at the upper end of the fire-place, both ends being alike plebeian. When a person of respectability enters, the father, moving towards the door, resigns his place to his guest, places skins under him, and otherwise pays every attention to his comfort. They are extremely hospitable, and cheerfully share their last morsel with the stranger who may be in want. Hospitality, however, is a virtue which civilization rarely improves.

A good hunter always leaves his lodge by dawn of day, and seldom tastes food till he returns late at night. Hunting beavers is a most laborious occupation, and becomes more so in proportion to the scarcity of these animals; for this reason, that when a great number of beavers occupy a lake, their places of retreat are in closer proximity to each other, and for the most part inhabited; if the number be reduced, it is likely they will have the same places of retreat, and the hunter must bore through the ice, before he can ascertain whether they are inhabited or not.

The sagacity of their dogs is truly surprising. The beaver house being first destroyed by the hunter, the dogs are urged by a peculiar call to scent out their retreats, which they never fail to do, whatever may be the thickness of the ice. They keep running about the borders of the lake, their noses close to the ground, and the moment they discover a retreat, begin to bark and jump on the ice; the hunter then cuts a hole with his trench, and with a stick which he carries along with him feels for the beaver; should he find one, he introduces his bare arm into the hole, and seizing his prey by the tail, drags it out on the ice, where it is dispatched with a spear. There is less danger in this operation than one would imagine, for the beaver allows itself to be seized without a struggle, but sometimes inflicts severe wounds on his captor after he is taken out of the water.

When the retreat is not inhabited, the entrance to it is barred by sticks, and the hunter proceeds to chisel again, and continues his operations until the beaver is either taken, or shut out from all his haunts, in which case he is compelled to return to the house to take breath, where he is either shot or caught in a trap.

The language of these Indians is a dialect of the Sauteux or Bungee, intermixed with Cree, and a few words of French derivation. The greater part of them have a smattering of French or English; but the acquisition of a foreign language is extremely difficult to them, from the peculiar formation of their own, which wants the letter r. An Algonquin pronounces the word "marrow" "manno" or "mallo." Their dialect has all the softness of the Italian, but is extremely poor and defective.

CHAPTER XV

On the 25th April, 1833, I embarked on board of a steamboat at Lachine, and reached Hull on the 27th. Here the regular conveyance by land carriages and steamboat ended, and the traveller in those days was obliged to wait his passage by the canoes of shanty men, or hire a boat or canoe for himself. I had recourse to the latter expedient, and reached the post of the Chats, then in charge of my esteemed friend Mr. McD——l, on the 30th. Captain Back arrived on the 1st of May, put ashore for a few supplies and my wards, and immediately re-embarked.

The brigade arrived on the 2d, and the guide delivered me a letter from Mr. K——, informing me that I was to consider myself merely as a passenger, the command of the men being entrusted to the guide by Governor Simpson's orders. This arrangement relieved me of much anxiety and trouble; though I would rather have preferred undergoing any personal inconvenience to being placed under the command of an ignorant Canadian, who might use his "brief" authority in a way very offensive to my feelings, without being guilty of anything that I could complain of.

My fears, however, were disappointed, as he showed every deference to my wishes, as well as the utmost courtesy to the other passengers, most of whom were of a rank not likely to find much consideration from a Canadian boatman; they consisted of a young priest not yet ordained, an apprentice clerk, three youths who had been at their education in Lower Canada, and myself.

The brigade consisted of three Montreal canoes, laden with provisions for the trip, and some tobacco for the southern department; and manned by sixty Iroquois and Canadians, the latter engaged to winter, the former for the trip.

The day was far spent when we left the portage of the Chats, and we encamped in the evening near the head of the rapids. The mode of travelling in canoes being now well known, I shall not detail the occurrences of each day, but confine myself to the narration of such incidents as may be most worthy of notice throughout the voyage. The moment we landed the tent was pitched by men employed for the purpose; the other men unloaded the canoes, and carried the goods beyond high-water mark, where it was piled and covered with oil-cloths.

It is the particular duty of the bowsman to attend to the canoe, to repair and pitch it when necessary, and to place it in security when the cargo is discharged. In consideration of these services he is exempt from the duty of loading or unloading, his wages are higher than those of the steersman, and he ranks after the guide. The latter generally messes with the gentlemen, his canoe always takes the lead in the rapids, but in still water the post of honour is held by the best going canoe. The guide rouses the men in the morning; the moment the call is heard, "Lève, lève!" the passengers spring upon their feet, tie up their beds, and if they are not smart about it, the tents go down about their ears, and they must finish the operation in the open air.

Several of our men having already deserted, we encamped upon islands, when they could be found, or kept watch on the mainland. Our hour of departure was three o'clock, A.M.; when the weather permitted we breakfasted at seven, dined at one or two o'clock, P.M., and encamped at sunset. In calm weather the canoes went abreast, singing in chorus and keeping time with the paddles. All was then gaiety, and, to appearance, happiness; but this is one of those bright spots in a voyageur's life which are few and far between.

We reached Fort Coulonge on the 3d, and it being late, I took up my quarters with my worthy old bourgeois, Mr. S. Here we received some additional supplies of provisions for the crews and passengers. We arrived at Lac des Allumettes on the 5th, where I put ashore merely to say *bon jour* to an old acquaintance. We encamped rather early this evening, to allow the men a little extra rest, on account of the laborious duty they had performed for some days before. Next day, when ascending the rapid of Roche Capitaine, the canoe in which I was passenger came in violent contact with another; but mine only sustained damage. The bow being stove in, the canoe began to fill; we however gained the shore, to which fortunately we were close, at a leap, and lost no time in discharging the cargo. Drying the goods and repairing the canoe occupied us a good part of the day.

We reached the Forks of Mattawin on the 8th, where we found a small outpost belonging to the Fort Coulonge district, recently established for the purpose of securing the hunts of the Indians of this quarter, who were in the habit of trading with shanty men. Being no longer under any apprehensions of the men deserting, we now discontinued the watch and slept in comfort.

The passage of the Little River was effected with much toil and difficulty, from the shallowness of the water. We entered Lake Nipissing on the 10th; descended French River, a rapid and dangerous stream, without accident, and entered Lake Huron on the morning of the 12th. The guide pointed out to me a place near the mouth of the river where the Indians used to waylay the canoes on their passage to and from the interior; a sort of rude breastwork still marks the spot. After much destruction of life and property by the savages, they were eventually caught in their own toil; the voyageurs, instead of descending the river at this place, passed by land, and coming unawares on the Indians killed them all.

We reached the post of the Cloche early on the 13th, and spent two hours in the company of Mr. McB— —u, who entertained us most kindly; and on the 14th looked in at Mississaga post, an establishment which appeared to possess but few attractions as a place of residence; consisting of a few miserable log buildings, surrounded by a number of pine-bark wigwams, the temporary residence of the natives; several of whom came reeling into the house after our arrival, there being an opposition party there.

These Indians were, without comparison, the most uncouth, savage-looking beings I ever beheld; mouth from ear to ear, cheek-bones remarkably high, low projecting forehead, hair like a horse's mane, and eyes red and swollen by continual intoxication. American whisky had no doubt contributed to increase their natural deformity.

After leaving this post we had a strong breeze of adverse wind for the remainder of the day, and encamped in consequence earlier than usual. On the following morning we were very early roused from our slumbers by the call of "Canot à lège," (light canoe). Our beds were tied up, tents packed, canoes launched and loaded in an instant; and we set off in pursuit of the mail, which we overtook at breakfast time, and found Mr. G. K— —th in charge, who had just returned from England, and was now proceeding to assume the charge of Lake Superior district. Mr. K— —th exchanged some of his men, who were found incapable of performing light canoe duty, for some of our best; an arrangement that did not appear to please our guide much.

The duty which the crew of a light canoe have to perform is laborious in the extreme, and requires men of the greatest strength and vigour to stand it. They are never allowed to remain more than four hours ashore by night, often only two or three; during the day they are constantly urged on by the guide or person in command, and never cease paddling, unless during the few moments required to exchange seats, or while they take their hasty meals ashore. They are liberally plied with grog, well paid, and well fed, and seldom quit the service until it is hinted to them that the duty is become too hard for them. A light canoe-man considers it quite a degradation to be employed in loaded craft.

We arrived early on the 16th at the Company's establishment at Sault Sainte Marie, where there is a large depot of provisions for the purpose of supplying the canoes passing to and from the interior and the surrounding districts. The south side of the river is occupied by the Americans as a military post, and it was gratifying to see the friendly intercourse that subsisted between the American officers and the gentlemen in the Company's service. Would that the same good feeling were more universal between two nations of one blood and the same language!

The rapid which unites the waters of Lakes Huron and Superior is avoided by making a portage. The carrying of the canoes and goods to the upper end of this portage occupied the men till about noon, when we embarked on the "Sea of Canada," having Messrs. Bethune and McKenzie on board as passengers. We proceeded about fifteen miles and encamped. We were ready to embark at the usual hour next morning, but being prevented by the high wind, to make the best of the time we turned in again, and after a most refreshing nap got up to breakfast.

The weather moderating soon after, all hands were ordered to embark, but all hands were not there; four of them had deserted during the night, and were not missed until the crews mustered for embarkation.

While we were holding a consultation regarding this unpleasant matter, an Indian canoe luckily cast up, and it was determined to despatch a party of Iroquois, conducted by a passenger in disguise, in pursuit of the fugitives. Another party was sent by land, and after an absence of about three hours returned with their prisoners. No criminals ever appeared more dejected than they; so humble did they seem, that they got off with a slight reprimand.

We reached the post of Michipikoton early on the morning of the 19th, and passed the remainder of the day waiting for despatches which Mr. K— — was preparing for the interior. We left on the 20th, put ashore at the Pic on the 23d, where we dined with Mr. McMurray, and after experiencing much bad weather, adverse winds, together with showers of snow, we reached Fort William on the 28th, about noon.

We found the grand depot of the North-West Company falling rapidly to decay, presenting in its present ruinous state but a shadow of departed greatness. It is now occupied as a petty post, a few Indians and two or three old voyageurs being the sole representatives of the crowded throngs of former times. It must have been a beautiful establishment in its days of prosperity; but the buildings certainly do not appear to have been erected with a view to durability. We here exchanged our large Montreal canoes for those of the North, (the former carrying seventy packages of ninety pounds, the latter twenty-five, exclusive of provisions;) and each of the passengers had a canoe for his own accommodation—an arrangement that seemed to increase in no small degree the self-importance of some of our number. Our guide was now obliged to perform the duty of bowsman, still, however, retaining his authority over the whole brigade.

We bade adieu to Fort William and its hospitable commander on the 29th. Mr. McI— —h had supplied all our wants most liberally, but the men were now allowed only Indian corn and a small quantity of grease;—a sad and unpleasing change for poor Jean Baptiste; but he had no help but to submit, though not perhaps with the utmost "Christian resignation."

Our men being now well disciplined, and our canoes comparatively light, we sped over our way at an excellent rate. We encamped on the 4th of June at one of the Thousand Lakes, and the canoes were drawn up before M. Thibaud (the priest) arrived. I was surprised to observe his frowning aspect on landing, and ascribed it to the circumstance of his being the "harse," or harrow, a term of derision applied to the slowest canoe. Calling me aside, however, he explained the cause of his discontent, which was very different from what I had surmised: his crew, whenever they found themselves sufficiently far in the rear to be out of hearing, invariably struck up an obscene song, alike unmindful of his presence and remonstrances; and this day had not only sung, but indulged in conversation the most indecent imaginable. This announcement appeared to me the more strange, that most of these young men had never before quitted home; and I had always understood the authority of the priest to be, at least, equal to that of the parent. Although, therefore, I never had any very great reverence for the (so-called) successors of St. Peter, I yet felt for my fellow-traveller, and addressed the miscreants who had insulted him in terms of grave reprehension, threatening them with severe punishment if such conduct should again be repeated.

We arrived at the post of Lac de la Pluie, on the 8th of June; and, after a short halt, and carrying our *impedimenta* across the portage on which the fort is situated, commenced the descent of Lac de la Pluie river,—a beautiful stream, running with a smooth, though strong current, and maintaining a medium breadth of about 200 yards. Its banks, which are clothed with verdure to the water's edge, recede by a gradual slope until they terminate in a high ridge, running parallel to the river on both sides. This ridge yields poplar, birch, and maple, with a few pines, proving the excellence of the soil. The interior, however, is said to be low and swampy.

We passed the residence of an old retired servant of the Company, on the 9th, who, if I may judge from the appearance of his farm and the number of his cattle, must vegetate very much at his ease.

Observing in the evening a large Indian camp, I requested the guide to put ashore for a little. We were received kindly, but in a manner quite different to what I had been accustomed. The young men were drawn up on the shore, and eyed us with a savage *fierté* in their looks, returning our salutation in a way that convinced us that we were at length among the "wild men of the woods." The weather being extremely hot, we found them in almost a complete state of nudity, with only a narrow shred of cloth around their loins. They speak the Sauteux language; and I had much difficulty in making myself understood by them. In their physiognomy and personal appearance they exhibit all the characteristic features of the genuine aboriginal race; and this party certainly appeared, one and all, to be "without a cross;" but there had been long a trading post at Lac la Pluie, and I noticed, in a neighbouring camp, a lass with brown hair and pretty blue eyes. Where did she get them? After bartering some sturgeon with the Indians, and presenting them with a little tobacco, we parted good friends, and encamped so near them as to be annoyed the whole night by the sound of their drum.

On the following morning we entered the Lake of the Woods, and next morning White River, a very violent stream, full of falls and dangerous rapids. The portages are innumerable, and often close together. After crossing one of these portages, we observed, with astonishment, a number of people on the next portage, La Cave, about pistol-shot distance from us. They proved to be Mr. Hughes, formerly partner of the North-West Company; Mr. Berens, a member of Committee, and suite: they were painfully situated, in consequence of the loss of their bowsman, who, by missing a stroke with his pole, fell into the rapid, and was drowned: the steersman was saved with great difficulty.

We got safe through this dangerous river, on the 15th; but two of the men had a narrow escape in one of the last portages. Our guide here, as everywhere else, having a picked crew, pushed on, and left us considerably in the rear. Approaching a fall, Le Bonnet, where no traces of a portage could be discovered, the men unloaded the canoes, and commenced carrying the goods through the woods; but the *boutes* (bowsmen and steersmen) determined on wading down with the canoes, the water being shallow, until they should come close to the fall; where, by lifting them across a narrow point, they could place them in the smooth water beneath. The attempt was made accordingly, by the leading canoe; but the rock over which the current flows being smooth, and covered with a slimy moss, the men slipped, and were in an instant precipitated over the fall. When we saw the canoe rushing over the brink, with the poor fellows clinging to it, we all concluded they had reached the end of their voyage. Running down to the foot of the fall, which was about eleven feet high, having previously ordered a canoe to be carried across the point, and some shots to be fired to recall the guide, who was now nearly out of sight, I was astonished to find the canoe had not upset, although the men had got into it, and it was half full of water, and so near the shore that I extended my arm to lay hold of the bow. The next moment, however, the stern having come within the influence of a whirlpool, it was hurried out into the middle of the stream, and dashed with such violence against a rock, that the crashing of the timbers was distinctly heard from the shore. This shock, which had nearly proved fatal to the men, threw the canoe into an eddy, or counter-current, which whirled it to the opposite shore, where it was about to sink when assistance came.

In the evening, we arrived at the post of Bas de la Rivière, in charge of an Orkney-man, by name Clouston, who had risen from the ranks, and who, seeing what small fry he had to deal with, treated us somewhat superciliously. Our stock of provisions being exhausted, we applied to *Maister* Clouston for a fresh supply: he granted us what I thought very inadequate to our wants; but he said it was all that was allowed by the Governor for the passage of the Lake. Here M. Thibaud found two men with a small canoe, who had been sent by the Bishop of Red River to convey him to his destination, waiting his arrival. We parted with feelings of mutual regret.

We left this post late on the 16th, and had proceeded but a short distance on the Lake, when a strong head wind compelled us to put ashore. We now experienced constant bad weather, never completing a day's sailing without interruption from some cause or other; and in consequence of these delays, it was found necessary to curtail our allowance of provisions. On the 20th, we pitched our tents near a camp of Sauteux, from whom the men procured a small quantity of sturgeon, in exchange for some articles of clothing. I was surprised to find Indians, in a quarter so remote from those tribes with whom I had hitherto been conversant, speaking a dialect which I understood perfectly: their erratic habits, and intercourse with the Crees and Algonquins, may perhaps account for this similarity of dialect.

I entered into conversation with a shrewd old fellow, who had been often at Red River settlement. Among other questions, I asked him whether he had not been baptized?

"Baptized!" he exclaimed; "don't speak of it, my brother. Baptized— that I may go to the devil! Indians think a good Indian goes to the good place when he dies; but the priests send *all* to the evil one."

I asked him how he made that out?

"Why, I learned it from the priests themselves. When I first went to Red River, I met a French priest, who earnestly besought me to be converted. I heard him attentively, and his words had a great effect upon me; but I had been told there was another priest there, who had different thoughts about religion, and I thought I would go to him too. He was very kind to me, and spoke nearly the same words as the French priest; so that I thought there was no difference in their religions. He asked me if I would be baptized? and I told him that I would; but I wanted to learn the French prayer. 'Ah! my son,' he said, 'that must not be: if you adopt that bad religion, you will be burned for certain.' And he spoke so strong, that I almost thought he was right. But before I would do anything, I went to the French priest again, and told him what the English priest said to me; and then said I would learn the English prayer. 'Ah! my son,' said he, 'if you do so, it will lead you to perdition: all that pray after the English manner go to the fire.' And he said much more, and his words were very strong too; so I saw that I could be no better by forsaking the belief of my fathers, and I have not gone to French or English priest since."

This is by no means a solitary case; and it is one of the sore evils which arise from the corruption of Christianity, and the divisions of Christians. Nor, in the case of creeds so opposite as those of Protestants and Roman Catholics—creeds as opposite as light and darkness—is it easy to point out a remedy. After all, it is surely better for these poor Indians to adopt some form of Christianity, however corrupt, than to remain in the darkness and debasement of heathenism. And if our missionaries would act upon the noble maxim of the greatest of the Apostles—"never to enter upon the sphere of another man's labours,"—consequences so injurious would be avoided. If they have not so much Christianity and good sense as to do so of themselves, where there is the power, they should be compelled to do it. The Company have the power, but are too much occupied with matters which they deem more momentous, to waste a thought upon this.

CHAPTER XVI

High winds detained us in camp on the 21st. The crews of two canoes, having finished their last meal to-day, bartered some more of their clothes for dogs. We reached a small outpost called Berens House on the 23d, where we procured a couple of sturgeon, and a dog valued at ten shillings, for which I gave my note of hand. I had a *preein* of this cynic mutton at breakfast; and could not help thinking it would have made a most appropriate and *philosophical* addition to the larder of the wise man of the tub. The men, however, having been for some time on short commons, seemed to relish it. We supped lightly enough on the remainder of Mr. Clouston's bountiful supply, giving a share to the men.

After a most tedious and miserable passage, we reached the outlet of Lake Winnipeg on the 24th, and arrived next morning at Norway House. Here the men were liberally supplied; and I found myself at breakfast with a number of chief factors and chief traders, just arrived from their respective districts, and on their way with their valuable returns to York Factory. Captain Back was also here, having sent on his men and baggage under the command of Dr. King, intending himself to follow in a light canoe, after having forwarded his despatches to Europe.

The day after my arrival, I was notified by one of the officials, that it was arranged that I should pass the summer here, giving such assistance to the gentleman in charge as might be required of me; and that my future destination should be determined upon at York Factory. I now passed my time very agreeably, having just enough employment in the day-time to keep off *ennui*, and the company of several gentlemen, and, what I thought still better, that of a fair countrywoman,14 in the evening. I was gratified to find that there existed here a far greater degree of intimacy between gentlemen of different ranks in the service, than in the Montreal department, where a clerk is considered as a mere hireling; here, on the contrary, commissioned officers look upon clerks as candidates for the same rank which themselves hold, and treat them accordingly.

The Governor, having taken up his residence for some years past in England, crosses the Atlantic once a year, and during his brief sojourn, Norway House forms his head-quarters. Here it is that the sham Council is held, and everything connected with the business of the interior arranged.

Here also is the depot for the districts of Athabasca and McKenzie's River, which supplies all the provisions required for inland transport. These provisions are furnished by the Saskatchewan district, or are purchased by the Company from the colonists of Red River, who have no other customers.

The natives of this quarter speak a jargon of Cree and Sauteux, which sounds very harshly. They all understand English, and some of them speak it fluently. Many of them are constantly employed as voyageurs between Norway House and York Factory; and none perform the trip more expeditiously, or render their cargoes in better condition than they. Of Christianity, they have learned just as much as enables them to swear; in other respects, they are still Pagans.

On the 20th of July, I received a letter from Mr. Chief Factor Cameron, who acted as President of the Council in the Governor's absence, conveying orders for me to proceed to New Caledonia; Mr. Charles being instructed to furnish me with a passage to Athabasca, and to forward me afterwards to Fort Dunvegan, on Peace River, where I was to wait the arrival of the party sent annually from New Caledonia for a supply of leather.

The brigade having been despatched on the 27th, Mr. C. and I embarked on the 28th, and overtook it at the entrance of Lake Winnipeg. The crews being ashore, and enjoying themselves, we passed on; hut did not proceed far, ere the wind blew so violently as to compel us to put ashore. After a delay of about four hours, we "put to sea" again; and the wind gradually abating as we proceeded, we encamped in the evening nearly opposite to McIntosh's Island.

This island, some years ago, presented an extensive surface of land covered with wood: there is not now a vestige of land to be seen; the spot where it existed being only known to voyagers by a shoal which is visible at low water. But not only have the islands been swept away, but the mainland along the west end of the lake seems gradually being encroached upon and engulphed by the waves; an undeniable proof of which is, that the old post of Norway House, which formerly stood at a considerable distance from the water's edge, is now close to it, and the burial-ground is nearly all submerged.

We arrived at the foot of Grand Rapid late on the 29th of July, and passed the portage on the 30th, assisted by the natives—Sauteux, Crees, and half-breeds. These live luxuriously on sturgeon, with little toil. Among them I observed two or three old Canadians, who could scarcely be distinguished from the natives by language, manners, or dress; such persons, when young, having formed an attachment to some of the Indian young women, betake themselves to their half-savage mode of life, and very soon cannot be persuaded to quit it.

We arrived on the 5th of August at Rivière du Pas, where an old Canadian, M. Constant, had fixed his abode, who appeared to have an abundance of the necessaries of life, and a large family of half-Indians, who seemed to claim him as their sire. We breakfasted sumptuously on fish and fowl, and no charge was made; but a gratuity of tea, tobacco, or sugar is always given; so that M. Constant loses nothing by his considerate attentions to his visitors.

We reached Cumberland House on the 8th. Here I was cheered by the sight of extensive corn-fields, horned cattle, pigs and poultry, which gave the place more the appearance of a farm in the civilized world, than of a trading post in the far North-West; and I could not help envying the happy lot of its tenant, and contrasting it with my own, which led me to the wilds of New Caledonia—to fare like a dog, without knowing how long my exile might be protracted.

We arrived at the post of Isle à la Crosse, where we were detained a day in consequence of bad weather. This post is also surrounded by cultivated fields, and I observed a few cattle; but the voice of the grunter was not heard.

The Indians who frequent this post are chiefly Chippeweyans, with a few families of Crees. The former differ in features, language, and manners from any I had yet seen. Their face is of a peculiar mould, broad; the cheekbone remarkably prominent, chin small, mouth wide, with thick lips, the upper covered with beard; the body strongly built and muscular. They appear destitute of the amiable qualities which characterise the Crees. Whenever we met any of them on our route, and asked for fish or meat, "Budt hoola,"[15] was the invariable answer; yet no Indians were ever more importunate than they in begging for tobacco. On the contrary, when we fell in with Crees, they allowed us to help ourselves freely, and were delighted to see us do so, receiving thankfully whatever we gave them in return. The features of the Crees are not so strongly marked as those of the Sauteux, although they are a kindred people; yet they are as easily distinguishable from each other, as an Englishman from a Frenchman.

We left Isle à la Crosse on the 12th, and without meeting with any adventure worthy of notice, reached the end of Portage la Loche about two o'clock P.M. of the following day, with canoe and baggage. In this, as in every other part of their territories, the Company use boats for the transport of property; but by a very judicious arrangement, much time and labour are saved at this portage, which is said to be twelve miles in length. Boats are placed at the upper and lower ends, so that the men have only to carry across the property, which, in truth, of itself is a sufficiently laborious operation for human beings. The people from the district of McKenzie's River come thus far with their returns, and receive their outfit in boats manned by half-breeds, who are hired at Red River for the trip.

The prospect which the surrounding country presents from the upper end of the portage is very striking; and the more so from the sudden manner in which it bursts upon the view. You suddenly arrive at the summit of a remarkably steep hill, where, on looking around, the first object that attracts attention is a beautiful green hill standing on the opposite side of the deep glen, through which the clear Water River flows, forming the most prominent feature of an extensive range, cut up by deep ravines, whose sides are clothed with wood, presenting already all the beautiful variety of their autumnal hues; while, at intervals, a glimpse was caught of the river meandering through the valley. In former times these hills were covered with herds of buffaloes, but not one is to be seen now.

We once more proceeded down the stream, and arrived at Athabasca on the 21st of August, where we found Dr. King, who had been delayed some days repairing his boats; Capt. Back having proceeded onwards in a light canoe to fix on a winter residence.

Fort Chippeweyan was, in the time of the North-West Company, next in importance to Fort William. Besides having several detached posts depending immediately upon itself, and carrying on a very extensive trade with the Chippeweyans, (the best hunters in the Indian country,) it served as depôt for the districts of McKenzie's River, and Peace River.

The trade of this district, although it bears no comparison to that of former times, is yet pretty extensive. It is still the depôt for Peace River, and commands the trade with the Chippeweyans. Trade is carried on in this quarter solely by barter, which secures the Company from loss, and is apparently attended with no inconvenience to the natives, who used formerly to take their supplies on credit.

Beaver is the standard according to which all other furs are rated; so many martens, so many foxes, &c., equal to one beaver. The trader, on receiving the Indian's hunt, proceeds to reckon it up according to this rule, giving the Indian a quill for each beaver; these quills are again exchanged at the counter for whatever articles he wants. The people of this post subsist entirely on the produce of the country, fish, flesh, and fowl, of which there is the greatest abundance. Both soil and climate are said to be unfavourable to the cultivation of grain or vegetables; the attempt is made, however, and sometimes with success.

I took my departure from Athabasca on the 24th of August, accompanied by Mr. Charles Ross, who had passed the summer there as *locum tenens*, and was now proceeding to assume the charge of his own post, Fort Vermillion, where we arrived on the 1st of September.

This post is agreeably situated on the right bank of Peace River, having the river in front, and boundless prairies in the rear. The Indians attached to it are designated Beaver Indians, and their language is said to have some affinity to the Chippeweyan. This is, however, the only point of resemblance between them. The Beavers are a more diminutive race than the Chippeweyans, and their features bear a greater resemblance to those of the Crees. They are allowed to be generous, hospitable and brave; and are distinguished for their strict adherence to truth.

Most Indians boast of the murder of white men as a glorious exploit; these, on the contrary, glory in never having shed the blood of one, although they often imbrue their hands in the blood of their kindred; being very apt to quarrel among themselves, chiefly on account of their gallantry. When an illicit amour is detected, the consequence is frequently fatal to one of the parties; but the unmarried youth, of both sexes, are generally under no restraint whatever.

I bade adieu to Mr. Ross, a warm-hearted Gael, on the 3d, and arrived at Fort Dunvegan on the 10th of September, then under the charge of Mr. McIntosh, chief factor, where I met with a Highland welcome, and passed the time most agreeably in the company of a well educated gentleman. The Indians here are of the same tribe as those of Fort Vermillion, but are not guiltless of the blood of the whites. This post is also surrounded by prairies. A large farm is cultivated, yielding in favourable seasons a variety of vegetables and grain: but the crops are subject to injury from frost; sometimes are altogether destroyed. When the wind blows for some time from the west, it cools in its passage across the glaciers of the Rocky Mountains, to such a degree, that the change of temperature caused by it is not only severely felt in the vicinity of the mountains, but at a great distance from them, as far even as Red River.

From the great age attained by many of the retired servants of the Company, who pass their lives in this country, the salubrity of the climate may fairly be inferred. Meeting a brigade of small canoes between Fort Vermillion and this place, and observing an old man with a white head and wrinkled face, sitting in the centre of one of them, I made up to him, and after saluting him *(à la Française,* presented him with a piece of tobacco—the

Indian letter of introduction. I inquired of him how long it was since he had left home.

"Sixty-two years, Monsieur," was the reply; and as the canoes assembled around us, he pointed out to me his sons, and his sons' sons, to the third and fourth generation.

I heard of no malady which the white inhabitants are liable to, except the goîtres; caused, it is presumed, in part by the use of snow-water, and in part by the use of the river-water, which is strongly impregnated with clay, so much so, as sometimes to resemble a solution of the earth itself.

Footnote 14: Mistress of the establishment.

Footnote 15: There is none.

CHAPTER XVII

Mr. Paul Fraser, a senior clerk, arrived from Caledonia with three canoes, on the 26th of September, and on the 28th we took our departure. Above Fort Dunvegan the current becomes so strong that the canoes are propelled by long poles, in using which the men had acquired such dexterity that we made much better progress than I could have expected. As we ascended the river, the scenery became beautifully diversified with hill and dale and wooded valleys, through which there generally flowed streams of limpid water. I observed at one place a tremendous land-slip, caused by the water undermining the soil. Trees were seen in an inverted position, the branches sunk in the ground and the roots uppermost; others with only the branches appearing above ground; the earth rent and intersected by chasms extending in every direction; while piles of earth and stones intermixed with shattered limbs and trunks of trees, contributed to increase the dreadful confusion of the scene. The half of a huge hill had tumbled into the river, and dammed it across, so that no water escaped for some time. The people of Dunvegan, seeing the river suddenly dry up, were terrified by the phenomenon, but they had not much time to investigate the cause: the river as suddenly reappeared, presenting a front of nearly twenty feet in height, and foaming and rushing down with the noise of thunder.

On the 3d of October we reached the tenantless Fort of St. John's, where a horrid tragedy was enacted some years ago—the commander of the post with all his men having been cut off by the Indians. The particulars of this atrocious deed, as related to me by the gentleman at the head of the district at the time, were as follows:—

It had been determined that the post of St. John's should be abandoned, and the establishment removed to the Rocky Mountain portage, for the convenience of the Tsekanies, who were excellent hunters, but who could not be well supplied from this post, on account of the greatness of the distance. Unfortunately a quarrel had arisen about this time between the Indians of St. John's and the Tsekanies. The former viewed the removal of the post from their lands as an insult, and a measure that gave their enemies a decided superiority over them, and they took a very effectual method of disappointing them.

Mr. Hughes, having sent off his men with a load of property for the new post, remained alone. This was the opportunity the Indians sought for, and they did not fail to take advantage of it. The unfortunate man had been in the habit of walking daily by the river side, and was taking his usual promenade the day after the departure of his men, when he was shot down by two of the assassins. They then carried his body to his room and left it, and his blood still marks the floor. The men, altogether unconscious of the fate that awaited them, came paddling toward the landing-place, singing a voyageur's song, and just as the canoe touched the shore a volley of bullets was discharged at them, which silenced them for ever. They were all killed on the spot. The post has remained desolate ever since. Fort Dunvegan was also abandoned for some years, which reduced the natives to the greatest distress.

As soon as intelligence was received of the catastrophe, a party of half-breeds and Crees, under the command of one of the clerks, was fitted out in order to inflict deserved punishment on the murderers; but just as the party had got on the trail, and within a short distance of the camp, they received orders from the superintendent to return.

These orders were no doubt dictated by feelings of humanity, as Mr. McIntosh had learned that some Indians, who were not concerned in the murder, were in the same camp, and he was apprehensive the innocent might be involved in the same punishment with the guilty. The most of them, however, were afterwards starved to death; and the country having been abandoned by the Company, gave the natives occasion to remark, that the measure was dictated more by fear of them than by motives of humanity.

The Rocky Mountains came in view on the 8th of October, and we reached the portage bearing their name on the 10th, the crossing of which took us eight days, being fully thirteen miles in length, and excessively bad road, leading sometimes through swamps and morasses, then ascending and descending steep hills, and for at least one-third of the distance so obstructed by fallen trees as to render it all but impassable. I consider the passage of this portage the most laborious duty the Company's servants have to perform in any part of the territory; and, as the voyageurs say, "He that passes it with his share of a canoe's cargo may call himself a man."

In the passage we came upon a large camp of Tsekanies, Mr. Eraser's customers. Their dialect is similar to that of the Beaver Indians, but they understand the Cree, which is the medium of communication between Mr. F. and them. It thus appears that this language is understood from the shores of Labrador to the foot of the Rocky Mountains.

After passing the portage, the Rocky Mountains reared their snow-clad summits all around us, presenting a scene of gloomy grandeur, that had nothing cheering in it. One scene, however, struck me as truly sublime. As we proceeded onward the mountains pressed closer on the river, and at one place approached so near that the gap seemed to have been made by the river forcing a passage through them. We passed in our canoes at the base of precipices that rose almost perpendicularly above us on either side to the height of 3,000 or 4,000 feet! After passing through these magnificent portals, the mountains recede to a considerable distance, the space intervening between them and the river being a flat, yielding timber of a larger growth than I expected to find in such a situation.

We arrived at McLeod's Lake—Mr. Fraser's post—on the 25th, where a number of Indians were waiting their supplies. They received us quite in a military style, with several discharges of fire-arms, and appeared delighted at the arrival of their chief. They seemed to be on the best possible terms together—the white chief and his *red "tail"*. They are Tsekanies, and are reputed honest, industrious, and faithful.

The outfit for this post is conveyed on horse-back from Stuart's Lake. A more dreary situation can scarcely be imagined, surrounded by towering mountains that almost exclude the light of day, and snow storms not seldom occurring, so violent and long continued as to bury the establishment. I believe there are few situations in the country that present such local disadvantages; but there is the same miserable solitude everywhere; and yet we find natives of England, Scotland, and Ireland devoting their lives to a business that holds forth such prospects! I remained with my new friend one day, enjoying the comforts of his *eyry*, and then set off for the goal of my long course, where I arrived on the 28th of October.

CHAPTER XVIII

Fort St. James, the depôt of New Caledonia district, stands near the outlet of Stuart's Lake, and commands a splendid view of the surrounding country. The lake is about fifty miles in length, and from three to four miles in breadth, stretching away to the north and north-east for about twenty miles; the view from the Fort embraces nearly the whole of this section of it, which is studded with beautiful islands. The western shore is low, and indented by a number of small bays formed by wooded points projecting into the lake, the back-ground rising abruptly into a ridge of hills of varied height and magnitude. On the east the view is limited to a range of two or three miles, by the intervention of a high promontory, from which the eye glances to the snowy summits of the Rocky Mountains in the distant back-ground. I do not know that I have seen anything to compare with this charming prospect in any other part of the country; its beauties struck me even at this season of the year, when nature having partly assumed her hybernal dress, everything appeared to so much greater disadvantage.

The Indian village is situated in a lovely spot at the outlet of the lake, and consists of only five or six houses, but every house is occupied by several families. These buildings are of a very slight and simple construction, being merely formed of stakes driven into the ground; a square piece of timber runs horizontally along the top of this wall, to which the stakes are fastened by strips of willow bark. This inclosure, which is of a square form, is roofed in by placing two strong posts at each gable, which support the ridge pole, on which the roof sticks are placed, one end resting on the ridge pole, and the other on the wall, the whole being covered with pine bark: there is generally a door at each end, which is cut in the wall after the building is erected. These apertures are of a circular form, and about two and a half feet in diameter, so that a stranger finds it very awkward to pass through them. In effecting a passage you first introduce a leg, then bending low the body you press in head and shoulders; in this position you will have some difficulty in maintaining your equilibrium, for if you draw in the rest of the body too quickly, it is a chance but you will find yourself with your head undermost: the natives bolt through them with the agility of a weasel.

For some time after my arrival here, I had very little employment, there being a scribe already in the establishment, whose experience and industry required no assistance from me. I thus found myself a supernumerary—a character that did not suit me, but I was obliged to content myself for the present. We were joined early in winter by some of the gentlemen in charge of posts, when we managed to pass the time very agreeably. Mr. D——, superintendent of the district, played remarkably well on the violin and flute, some of us "wee bodies" could also do something in that way, and our musical soirees, if not in melody, could at least compete in noise, numbers taken into account, with any association of the kind in the British dominions. Chess, backgammon, and whist, completed the variety of our evening pastimes. In the daytime each individual occupied himself as he pleased. When together, smoking, "spinning yarns" about *dog* racing, canoe sailing, and *l'amour*; sometimes politics; now and then an animated discussion on theology, but without bitterness; these made our days fly away as agreeably as our nights.

While thus pleasantly occupied, a piece of intelligence was received, which caused the breaking up of our little society, and created some alarm. A party of seven or eight Indians having been drowned on their way to Alexandria, in autumn, their relatives imputed the misfortune to the whites. "Had there been no whites at Alexandria," said they, "our friends would not have gone there to trade; and if they had not gone there, they would not have been drowned:" *ergo*—the white men are the cause of their death, and the Indians must be avenged.

Nothing, however, was known of their hostile intentions until winter, when Mr. F. had occasion to send a man to Stuart's Lake with despatches, who, on arriving opposite to the Indian camp, found himself suddenly surrounded by the natives. They advanced rapidly upon him, brandishing their arms, and uttering horrid yells, and would have dispatched him on the spot but for the interference of one of themselves, who nobly threw himself between the Canadian and the muzzles of the guns that were levelled at him, and beckoned him to flee. He took to his heels accordingly, and never looked behind him till he reached the fort.

A little before Mr. Fisher had learned from his home guards that an attack on the fort was intended, and that they had been solicited by their neighbours to join in it, but had refused. So far, indeed, from wishing to injure the whites, they consented to carry the despatches which conveyed the information I have just mentioned. As Mr. F. urgently requested that assistance should be afforded him with as little delay as possible, it was determined that I should forthwith proceed to Alexandria, accompanied by Waccan, the interpreter, and eight men well armed.

Passing Fraser's Lake and Fort George posts, we arrived at the Indian winter camp, which we found abandoned; but a well beaten track led from it in the direction of Alexandria, a circumstance which made us apprehensive that our aid might come too late, and prompted us to redouble our speed. Our party consequently was soon very much scattered—a most unmilitary procedure—which might have proved fatal to ourselves, while we thought of relieving our friends.

The interpreter, myself, and two Iroquois, forming the advanced guard of the *grand army*, which consisted of full six men, still considerably in the rear, on turning a point found ourselves immediately in front of the camp. We were thus as much taken by surprise as those whom we wished to surprise; but without hesitating a moment we rushed up the bank, and were instantly in the midst of the camp. The uproar was tremendous, the Indians seized their arms with the most threatening gestures and savage yells, and it would have been impossible for us to execute our orders—which were to seize the ringleader only—without a fierce struggle and bloodshed on both sides; and though more resolute, perhaps, than our enemies, we were by far the weaker party, their numbers being at least ten to one of ours.

Happily, however, there was an Indian (one of our friends) from Alexandria, in the camp, who, as soon as he could make himself heard, informed us that the affair had been already arranged to the satisfaction of both parties. Thus terminated our expedition, without bloodshed and without laurels. A few days earlier it might have been otherwise; nor was Mr. F. without blame in neglecting to advise us of the arrangement.

We continued our course towards Fort Alexandria, and reached it late in the evening. My unexpected appearance gave my old bourgeois of Two Mountains an agreeable surprise. Having eaten nothing since morning, we made sad havoc of his beefsteaks and potatoes.

"Well, Mac," said he, "to judge from your appetite, the air of New Caledonia seems to agree wonderfully with you. Pray how do you like the beef-steaks?"

"Never tasted anything better," said I.

Next morning he requested me to accompany him to the store, as he said, to see a hind-leg of the steer which had furnished me with my steaks. I approached it, and lo! it was the hind-leg of a horse! The beef-steaks, or rather *horse*-steaks, were again presented at breakfast, and I confess I had not the same relish for them as at supper, but my repugnance—such is the effect of habit—was soon overcome.

I remained a few days here for the sake of repose, and then returned. On the approach of spring, my fellow-subordinate, Mr. McKenzie, dissatisfied with the service, left for the east side of the mountains, and I took his place at the desk, the duties of which, although by no means harassing, left me but little leisure. The accounts of all the posts in the district, eight in number, were made up here; I had also to superintend the men of the establishment, accompany them on their winter trips, and attend to the Indian trade. But even if the duty had been more toilsome, I had every inducement to perform it cheerfully, as Mr. Dease was one of the kindest and most considerate of men. On the 5th of May Mr. Dease took his departure for Fort Vancouver, with the returns of his district, which might he valued at 11,000*l*. The outfit, together with servants' wages and incidental expenses, amounted to about 3,000*l*., leaving to the Company a clear profit of about 8,000*l*.

I was appointed to the charge of Stuart's Lake during the summer, with four men to perform the ordinary duties of the establishment—making hay, attending to gardens, &c. A few cattle were introduced in 1830, and we now began to derive some benefit from the produce of the dairy. Our gardens (a term applied in this country to any piece of ground under cultivation) in former times yielded potatoes; nothing would now grow save turnips. A few carrots and cabbages were this year raised on a piece of new ground, which added to the luxuries of our table. Heaven knows, they were much wanted, for the other fare was scarcely fit for dogs! In the early part of the season it consisted entirely of salmon, which this year was of the worst quality, having been two years in the store. A few sturgeon, however, of enormous size, were caught, whose flesh was the most tender and delicious I had ever eaten, and would have been considered a delicacy by Apicius himself; it need not be wondered at then that the capture of one caused universal joy.

The salmon (the New Caledonian staff of life) ascend Frazer's River and its tributaries, from the Pacific in immense shoals, proceeding towards the sources of the streams until stopped by shallow water. Having deposited their spawn, their dead bodies are seen floating down the current in thousands; few of them ever return to the sea; and in consequence of the old fish perishing in this manner, they fail in this quarter every fourth year. The natives display a good deal of ingenuity in catching them. Where the current and depth of water permit, they bar it across by means of stakes driven into the bottom with much labour, and standing about six inches apart; these are strongly bound to a piece of timber, or "plate," running along the top; stays, or supporters, are placed at intervals of ten or twelve feet, the upper end bearing against the plate so as to form an angle with the stream. Gaps are left in the works of sufficient size to admit the *varveaux*, or baskets, in which the fish are taken. After the whole is finished, square frames of wicker-work, called keys, are let down against the upper side, to prevent the fish from ascending, and at the same time to allow the water a free passage. The keys must be kept entirely free from filth, such as branches, leaves, &c., otherwise the whole works would soon be swept away. The baskets are of a cylindrical form, about two and a half feet in diameter at the mouth, and terminate in a point of four or, five inches. When the fishing is over, all the materials are removed, and replaced the ensuing year with equal labour.

To preserve the fish for future consumption the following process is adopted. The back being split up, and the back-bone extracted, it is hung by the tail for a few days; then it is taken down and distended on splinters of wood; these are attached to a sort of scaffold erected for the purpose, where the fish remains till sufficiently dry for preservation. Even in dry seasons, during this process, the ground all round the scaffold is thickly covered with large maggots; but in wet seasons the sight becomes much more loathsome.

I have already observed that the salmon fail periodically, and the natives would consequently be reduced to the utmost distress, did not the goodness of Providence furnish them with a substitute. Rabbits are sent to supply the place of the salmon; and, singular as it may appear, these animals increase in number as the salmon decrease, until they swarm all over the country. When the salmon return, they gradually disappear, being destroyed or driven away by their greatest enemy, the lynx, which first appear in smaller, then in greater numbers;—both they and their prey disappearing together. As to the *cause* that induces those animals to appear and disappear in this manner, I cannot take upon myself to explain.

In the course of this summer one of our interpreters, a native, lost his life in rather a singular manner. He had made a bear-trap, and wishing to ascertain how it would work, tried his own weight on the spring, which yielded but too readily, and crushed him in so dreadful a manner that he only survived his experiment but a few hours. As he had withdrawn from the Company's service this year, his body was disposed of after the manner of his own people, except that it was buried instead of being burned; this, however, was the first instance of an interment, it being introduced through our influence in pity to the unfortunate widows, who are exposed to the cruellest tortures at the burning of the body. I never beheld a more affecting scene than the present. Immediately as the coffin was lowered into the grave, the widow threw herself upon it, shrieking and tearing her hair, and could only be removed by main force: several other females, relatives of the deceased, were also assembled in a group hard by, and evinced all the external symptoms of extreme grief, chanting the death-song in a most lugubrious tone, the tears streaming down their cheeks, and beating their breasts. The men, however, even the brothers of the deceased, showed no emotion whatever, and as soon as the rites were ended, moved off the ground, followed by the female mourners, who soon after were seen as gay and cheerful as if they had returned from a wedding. The widow, however, still remained by the grave, being obliged to do so in conformity with the customs of her nation, which required that she should mourn day and night, until the relatives of the deceased should collect a sufficiency of viands to make a feast in honour of his bones.

As already observed, the bodies were formerly burned; the relatives of the deceased, as well as those of the widow, being present, all armed; a funeral pile was erected, and the body placed upon it. The widow then set fire to the pile, and was compelled to stand by it, anointing her breast with the fat that oozed from the body until the heat became insupportable: when the wretched creature, however, attempted to draw back, she was thrust forward by her husband's relatives at the point of their spears, and forced to endure the dreadful torture until either the body was reduced to ashes, or she herself almost scorched to death. Her relatives were present merely to preserve her life; when no longer able to stand they dragged her away; and this intervention often led to bloody quarrels! The body being burned, the ashes were collected in a box and given in charge to the widow, who carried them about with her until the feast was prepared, when they were taken from her, and deposited in a small hut or placed upon the top of a wooden pillar neatly carved, as their final resting-place.

During this interval she was in a state of the most wretched slavery; every child in the village might command her and beat her unmercifully if they chose, no one interfered. After the feast, however, she regained her freedom, and along with that the privilege of incurring the risk of another scorching. Our interference relieved them from the most cruel part of the ceremony; the temporary state of slavery is still continued.

Footnote 16: Belluga?

CHAPTER XIX

Mr. Dease arrived from Fort Vancouver on the 5th of September, and expressed himself highly gratified with the appearance our "gardens" presented; an ample stock of salmon had also been laid in, so that we had nothing to fear from want, which sometimes had been severely felt. In the beginning of November, our despatches from the east side of the mountains came to hand, usually a joyful event, but saddened this year by the intelligence we received, that our excellent superintendent was about to leave us, having obtained permission to visit the civilized world for medical advice;—the doctor was only 5,000 miles off!

In the beginning of the winter we were invited to a feast held in honour of a great chief, who died some years before. The person who delivered the invitation stalked into the room with an air of vast consequence, and strewing our heads with down, pronounced the name of the presiding chief, and withdrew without uttering another syllable. To me the invitation was most acceptable: although I had heard much of Indian feasts, I never was present at any.

Late in the evening we directed our steps towards the "banqueting house," a large hut temporarily erected for the occasion. We found the numerous guests assembled and already seated around "the festive board;" our place had been left vacant for us, Mr. Dease taking his seat next to the great chief, Quaw, and we, his Meewidiyazees (little chiefs), in succession. The company were disposed in two rows: the chiefs and elders being seated next the wall, formed the outer, and the young men the inner row; an open space of about three feet in breadth intervening between them. Immense quantities of roasted meat, bear, beaver, siffleu or marmot, were piled up at intervals, the whole length of the building; berries mixed up with rancid salmon oil, fish roe that had been buried underground a twelve-month, in order to give it an *agreeable* flavour, were the good things presented at this feast of gluttony and flow of oil. The berry mixture, and roes were served in wooden troughs, each having a large wooden spoon attached to it. The enjoyments of the festival were ushered in with a song, in which all joined:—

"I approach the village,
Ya ha he ha, ya ha ha ha;

And hear the voices of many people,

Ya ha, &c.

The barking of dogs,

Ya ha, &c.

Salmon is plentiful,

Ya ha, &c.

The berry season is good,

Ya ha, &c.

After the song commenced the demolition of the mountains of meat, which was but slowly effected, notwithstanding the unremitting and strenuous exertions of the guests. The greatest order, however, was maintained; the relatives of the deceased acted as stewards, each of them seizing a roasted beaver, or something else, squatted himself in front of one of the guests, and presenting the meat, which he held with both his hands (males and females officiating), desired him to help himself. If the guest appeared backward in the attack, he was pressed, in the politest terms, to eat. "Now, I pray you, tear away with a good will;"—"I am glad to see you eat so strongly;"—"Come now, stuff yourself with this fine piece of fat bear." And stuff himself he must, or pay a forfeit, to avoid a catastrophe. But having paid thus, and acknowledged himself fairly overcome by his host's politeness, he is spared any further exertions, and his viands are no longer presented to him in this way, but placed in a dish beside him.

Well aware of our inability to maintain the honour of our country in a contest of this kind, we paid our forfeit at the commencement of the onslaught, reserving our portions to be disposed of at home.

The gormandizing contest ended as it began, with songs and dances; in the latter amusement, however, few were now able to join; afterwards ensued a rude attempt at dramatic representation. Old Quaw, the chief of Nekaslay, first appeared on the stage, in the character of a bear—an animal he was well qualified to personate. Rushing from his den, and growling fiercely, he pursued the huntsman, the chief of Babine portage, who defended himself with a long pole; both parties maintained a running fight, until they reached the far end of the building, where they made their exit. Enter afterwards a jealous husband and his wife, wearing masks (both being men). The part these acted appeared rather dull; the husband merely sat down by the side of his "frail rib," watching her motions closely, and neither allowing her to speak to nor look at any of the young men. As to the other characters, one personated a deer, another a wolf, a third a strange Tsekany. The bear seemed to give the spectators most delight.

The scene was interesting, as exhibiting the first rude attempts at dramatic representation of a savage people; and it served, in some measure, to efface the impression made by the somewhat disgusting spectacle previously witnessed. The affair concluded by an exchange of presents, and the party broke up.

Two young men, natives of Oregon, who had received a little education at Red River, had, on their return to their own country, introduced a sort of religion, whose groundwork seemed to be Christianity, accompanied with some of the heathen ceremonies of the natives. This religion spread with amazing rapidity all over the country. It reached Fort Alexandria, the lower post of the district, in the autumn; and was now embraced by all the Nekaslayans. The ceremonial consisted chiefly in singing and dancing. As to the doctrines of our holy religion, their minds were too gross to comprehend, and their manners too corrupt to be influenced by them. They applied to us for instruction, and our worthy chief spared no pains to give it. But, alas! it is for the most part labour in vain. Yet, an impression seemed to have been made on a few; and had there been missionaries there at the time, their efforts might have proved successful. But the influence of the "men of medicine," who strenuously withstand a religion which exposes their delusive tricks, and consequently deprives them of their gains,— together with the dreadful depravity everywhere prevalent,—renders the conversion of the Tekallies an object most difficult to accomplish.

It is a general opinion among Christians, that there exists no nation or people on earth who are entirely ignorant of a Supreme Being. I shall contrast the language of this tribe with that of the Sauteux or Ojibbeway, and let the reader judge for himself.

I have heard a heathen Ojibbeway, when giving a feast, express himself thus: "The great Master of Life, he who sees us and whom we cannot see, having done me charity, I invite you, my brother, to partake of it." On a like occasion, a Takelly describes the manner in which he killed his game, but never alludes to a deity. When an Ojibbeway wishes to confirm the truth of what he says beyond a doubt, he points to heaven and exclaims, "He to whom we belong hears that what I say is true." The Takelly says, "The toad hears me." You ask a Takelly what becomes of him after death, he replies, "My life shall be *extinct*, and I shall be dead." Not an idea has he of the soul, or of a future state of rewards and punishments. The Ojibbeway answers,

"After death my soul goes either to a happy land, abounding with game and every delight; or to a land of misery, where I shall suffer for ever from want. Whether it go to the good or bad place depends on my good or bad conduct here."

In fact the Takelly language has not a term in it to express the name of Deity, spirit, or soul. When the Columbia religion was introduced among them, our interpreters had to invent a term for the Deity—Yagasita—the "Man of Heaven." The only expression I ever heard them use that conveyed any idea whatever of a superior Being is, that when the salmon fail, they say, "The Man who keeps the mouth of the river has shut it up with his red keys, so that the salmon cannot get up." One of our gentlemen, a member of the Roman Catholic Church, teaching the Takellies to make the sign of the cross, with the words used on the occasion, his interpreter translated them, "Au nom du Père, de son Frère, et puis de son petit Garçon!" (In the name of the Father, his Brother, and his little Boy!)

The accompts and despatches for head-quarters being finished in the beginning of March, I was ordered to convey them to Fort Alexandria, to the charge of which post I was now appointed. This post is agreeably situated on the banks of Frazer's River, on the outskirts of the great prairies. The surrounding country is beautifully diversified by hill and dale, grove and plain; the soil is rich, yielding abundant successive crops of grain and vegetable, unmanured; but the crops are sometimes destroyed by frost. The charming locality, the friendly disposition of the Indians, and better fare, rendered this post one of the most agreeable situations in the Indian country. In spring, moreover, the country swarms with game—pheasants and a small species of curlieu in the immediate vicinity, and ducks and geese within a short distance. The sport was excellent, and, with the amusement the cultivation of my garden afforded me, enabled me to vegetate in great comfort—a comfort I was not destined long to enjoy.

Mr. Ogden, chief factor, arrived from Fort Vancouver about the end of May, and Mr. Fisher from Stuart's Lake a few days afterwards; and having consulted together, determined that I should retrace my steps to Stuart's Lake without delay. When I arrived at Fort St. James its dreadful solitude almost drove me to despair. I found myself sitting alone in the hall where my late excellent bourgeois and friends had passed the time so happily, and I felt a depression of spirits such as I never experienced before. Fortunately for me, my old friend Mr. Fraser, a gentleman of a gay and lively disposition, arrived soon after, and continued with me for the remainder of the season, and his company soon drove melancholy away.

The particulars of an affair which had occurred here some years before, and threatened the most serious consequences to the post, were about this time related to me by Waccan, the interpreter.

A native of Frazer's Lake had murdered one of the Company's servants, and, strange to say, no steps were taken to punish him; he concealed himself some time, and finding he had nothing to apprehend, returned to his village. At length he was led by his evil genius to visit Stuart's Lake, then under the command of a Douglas. Douglas heard of his being in the village, and though he had but a weak garrison, determined that the blood of the white man should not be unavenged. The opportunity was favourable, the Indians of the village were out on a hunting excursion, the murderer was nearly alone. He proceeded to the camp accompanied by two of his men, and executed justice17 on the murderer. On their return in the evening, the Indians learned what had happened, and enraged, determined to retaliate.

Aware, however, that Douglas was on his guard, that the gates were shut and could not be forced, they resolved to employ Indian stratagem.

The old chief accordingly proceeded to the Fort alone, and knocking at the gate desired to be admitted, which was granted. He immediately stated the object of his visit, saying that a deed had been done in the village which subjected himself and his people to a heavy responsibility to the relatives of the dead; that he feared the consequences, and hoped that a present would be made to satisfy them; and continuing to converse thus calmly, Mr. Douglas was led to believe that the matter could easily be arranged. Another knock was now heard at the gate: "It is my brother," said the chief, "you may open the gate; he told me he intended to come and hear what you had to say on this business."

The gate was opened, and in rushed the whole Nekasly tribe, the chief's brother at their head; and the men of the Fort were overpowered ere they had time to stand on their defence. Douglas, however, seized a wall-piece that was mounted in the hall, and was about to discharge it on the crowd that was pouring in upon him, when the chief seized him by the arms, and held him fast. For an instant his life was in the utmost peril. Surrounded by thirty or forty Indians, their knives drawn, and brandishing them over his head with frantic gestures, and calling out to the chief, "Shall we strike? shall we strike?"

The chief hesitated; and at this critical moment the interpreter's wife18 stepped forward, and by her presence of mind saved him and the establishment.

Observing one of the inferior chiefs, who had always professed the greatest friendship for the whites, standing in the crowd, she addressed herself to him, exclaiming, "What! you a friend of the whites, and not say a word in their behalf at such a time as this! Speak! you know the murderer deserved to die; according to your own laws the deed was just; it is blood for blood. The white men are not dogs; they love their kindred as well as you; why should they not avenge their murder?"

The moment the heroine's voice was heard the tumult subsided; her boldness struck the savages with awe; the chief she addressed, acting on her suggestion, interfered; and being seconded by the old chief, who had no serious intention of injuring the whites, was satisfied with showing them that they were fairly in his power. Mr. Douglas and his men were set at liberty; and an amicable conference having taken place, the Indians departed much elated with the issue of their enterprise.

A personal adventure of Waccan's is worth recording. An interpreter, a Cree half-breed, had been murdered by the Indians of Babine post with circumstances of great barbarity; and the perpetrators of the deed were allowed to exult in the shedding of innocent blood with impunity, one feeble, ineffectual attempt only having been made to chastise them. Waccan, however, determined that the matter should not end thus, the victim being his adopted brother. Having been sent to Babine post with an Indian lad, he learned from him that the murderers were encamped in a certain bay on Stuart's Lake, and resolved to seize the long wished-for opportunity of revenge; but fearing for his companion's safety more than his own, he landed him at a considerable distance from the camp, directing him to make the best of his way home if he should hear many shots.

He then paddled down as near the camp as he could without being discovered, and landing, threw off every article of clothing save a shred round his loins; and with his gun in the one hand, and dagger in the other, proceeded to the spot. Having approached sufficiently near to see all that passed in the encampment, he squatted among the bushes, and watching his opportunity, "picked off" the ringleader; then rushing from his covert, and giving the war whoop, he planted his dagger in his heart almost before the Indians had time to know what had happened. Seeing the infuriated "avenger of blood" in the midst of them, they fled precipitately to the woods. Waccan dared them to revenge the death of the "dead dog" who had murdered his brother.

"Come," said he, "you that were so brave at Babine Lake, and danced round the body of him whom you did not face, but knocked down when his back was to you, now is your time to show yourselves *men*.

No one answering the challenge, he shouldered his gun, walked along the beach to his canoe, and paddling leisurely off from the shore, sang the Cree song of triumph.

Footnote 17: "Wild justice," —BACON.

Footnote 18: This woman is the daughter of Mr. James MacDougal, a gentleman who had a chief hand in the settlement of the district. He served the Company for a period of thirty-five years, enduring all the hardships that were in his time inseparable from an Indian trader's life; and was dismissed from their service, in old age, without a pension, to starve on such little savings as he had effected out of his salary. He is still alive (1841), struggling with adversity.

CHAPTER XX

In the beginning of September, Mr. Ogden arrived from Fort Vancouver, and I was appointed by him to the charge of Fort George, whither I proceeded forthwith. Mr. Linton, my predecessor, was directed to wait the arrival of the party sent to Jasper's house for a supply of leather, ere he took his departure for Chilcotin, an outpost of Fort Alexandria.

Fort George was established a few years ago, and passed through the bloody ordeal ere yet the buildings were completed. The gentleman in charge, Mr. Yale, had left his men at work, and gone on a visit to Fort St. James, where he only remained a few days; on his return he found his men had been treacherously murdered by the Indians during his absence. Their mangled bodies were found in one of the houses, with one of their own axes by their side, which evidently had been the instrument of their destruction. The poor men were in the habit of retiring to rest during the heat of the day, and were despatched while they slept.

A great change has come over this people since that time; they are now justly considered the best disposed and most industrious Indians in the district. The situation of the post is exceedingly dreary, standing on the right bank of Frazer's River, having in front a high hill that shades the sun until late in the morning, and in the midst of "woods and wilds, whose melancholy gloom" is saddening enough. Yet it has its *agrémens*, its good returns,—the *ne plus ultra* of an Indian trader's happiness,—its good Indians, and its good fare; the produce of the soil and dairy.

Poor Linton had remained with me till late in autumn; when the cold weather setting in with unusual rigour, the ice began to drift on the river, rendering the navigation already dangerous; and no accounts having been received of the leather party, he determined to embark for his destination without further loss of time. He, alas! had already waited too long. Having occasion in the beginning of winter to send down a messenger to Fort Alexandria, I was surprised to see him two days after enter the fort, accompanied by one of Mr. Fisher's men, who brought me the melancholy tidings of Mr. L.'s death, part of his baggage having been found by the natives among the ice. Eight souls had perished, no one knows how; Mr. L., his wife and three children, an interpreter, his wife and one child.

Some suspicions attached to a disreputable family of Indians who were known to be encamped on the banks of the river at the time; but it is more probable that the catastrophe occurred in a rapid not far from this post, as a dog which the party had with them came back at an early hour the day after their departure. This misfortune threw a gloom over the whole district, where Linton was much beloved, and his death, so sudden and mysterious, made the blow be felt more severely.

Before this sad intelligence reached us, the safety of the leather party had become a source of deep anxiety. They had been expected in October, and no accounts had been received of them in the month of December. Having forwarded Mr. Fisher's despatches to head-quarters, I received orders from Mr. Ogden to proceed to Jasper's house, in order, if possible, to obtain information regarding them; which I eagerly obeyed, setting off with five men, and sledges loaded with provisions, drawn by dogs. We had not proceeded far, however, when we met the truants all safe and sound. Their non-arrival in the fall was occasioned by the winter setting in unprecedentedly early.

They experienced the utmost difficulty in crossing the Rocky Mountains, from the great depth of snow that had already fallen; and when they reached the heights of Frazer's River, they found the ice beginning to form along its shores. They persevered, however; sometimes forcing their way through the ice, sometimes carrying the canoes and property overland where the passage was blocked up by the ice. But all their efforts proved unavailing, for they were at length completely frozen in.

Their prospects were now most disheartening. Their remaining provisions would only suffice for four days on short allowance, and they had a journey of fifteen days before them, whichever way they should direct their course. Some of the men yielded to despair, but the greater part cheerfully embraced Mr. Andersen's views. Those only who are unacquainted with the Canadian voyageurs will deny them the possession of qualities, of the highest value in this country—ready obedience to their superiors, patience of fatigue and hardship, and unyielding perseverance under the most trying difficulties, so long as their leaders show them the way. Mr. Anderson having secured the property *en cache*, determined to return to Jasper's house, in order to procure at least a part of the much wanted supply of leather. On their way back they had the good fortune to light upon a stray horse, which they converted into provender: they also shot a moose deer; and thus providentially supplied, they suffered little from want.

On arriving at the post, they found to their sad disappointment that nothing could be got there, except some provisions; it was therefore necessary to proceed to Fort Edmonton, at least 400 miles distant, with but one intermediate post. They succeeded in reaching it, though in a most deplorable condition, half starved and half frozen, none of the party being provided with winter clothing; but they were most hospitably received by the kind-hearted bourgeois Mr. Rowand; and, after remaining a few days to recruit their strength in this land overflowing with fat and pemmican, and receiving their supplies, they set off on their return, and reached their destination without accident.

Farming on a small scale had been attempted here by my predecessor, and the result was such as to induce more extensive operations. I received orders, therefore, to clear land, sow and plant, forthwith. These orders were in part carried into effect in the autumn. Four acres of land were put in a condition to receive seed, and about the same quantity at Fort Alexandria. Seed was ordered from the Columbia, and handmills to grind our grain. Pancakes and hot rolls were thenceforward to be the order of the day; Babine salmon and dog's flesh were to be sent—"to Coventry!" The spring, however, brought with it but poor prospects for pancakes; the season was late beyond all precedent; the fields were not sown until the 5th of May; they, nevertheless, promised well for some time, but cold weather ensued, and continued so long that the crops could not recover before the autumn frosts set in, and thus our hopes were blasted. The farm at Alexandria had not much better success, owing to the neglect of the good people themselves;— not having enclosed their fields, the cattle destroyed the greater part of the crops. Here, however, notwithstanding the failure of our grain crops, we had abundance of vegetables and a large stock of cattle, so that our fare was far superior to that of the other *exiles* in the district.

Mr. Ogden returned from Fort Vancouver about the usual time, and was mortified to find that our grand agricultural experiment had so completely failed. He, however, had brought a supply of flour sufficient to afford each commander of posts a couple of bags, and thus the inconvenience arising from our disappointment was, in some degree, obviated.

From his first arrival amongst us, Mr. Ogden evinced the most earnest desire to ameliorate the condition of his subordinates in this wretched district, and all felt grateful to him for his benevolent intentions. To Mr. Dease, however, the praise is due of having introduced this new order of things: he it was who first introduced cattle from Fort Vancouver; it was he who first introduced farming, and recommended it to others.

Late in autumn, the natives being all about the post, the dread influenza, that had made such fearful havoc among the Indians in other quarters, broke out here also. The poor creatures had a great deal of confidence in my medical skill, from the circumstance of my having saved the life of a boy who had eaten some poisonous root, when despaired of by their own mountebanks.

On the present occasion I tried my skill on one of the subjects best able to bear my experiments, by administering a strong emetic and purge, and causing him afterwards to drink a decoction of mint. He was cured, and I afterwards prescribed the same medicine to many others with a like success; so that my reputation as a disciple of Æsculapius became firmly established.

Having last year applied to the Governor for permission to visit head-quarters, for a purpose which will be noticed hereafter, I received a favourable answer, and, in the month of February, set off for the depôt of the district preparatory to my departure, where I remained for a month in company with Mr. Ogden and several fellow-scribes.

CHAPTER XXI

Ere I proceed on my long journey, I must pause for a little to describe more particularly the country, which I am about to quit, perhaps for ever, and the manners of its savage inhabitants. The climate of New Caledonia is exceedingly variable at all seasons of the year. I have experienced at Stuart's Lake, in the month of July, every possible change of weather within twelve hours; frost in the morning, scorching heat at noon; then rain, hail, snow. The winter season is subject to the same vicissitudes, though not in so extreme a degree: some years it continues mild throughout. These vicissitudes may, I think, be ascribed to local causes—proximity to, or distance from the glaciers of the Rocky Mountains, the direction of the winds, the aspect of the place, &c. Fort St. James is so situated as to be completely exposed to the north-east wind, which wafts on its wings the freezing vapours of the glaciers. The instant the wind shifts to this quarter, a change of temperature is felt; and when it continues to blow for a few hours, it becomes so cold that, even in midsummer, small ponds are frozen over. The surrounding country is mountainous and rocky.

Frazer's Lake is only about thirty miles distant from Fort St. James (on Stuart's Lake), yet there they raise abundance of vegetables, potatoes and turnips, and sometimes even wheat and barley. The post stands in a valley open to the south-west,—a fine champaign country, of a sandy soil; it is protected from the north-east winds by a high ridge of hills. The winter seldom sets in before December, and the navigation is generally open about the beginning of May.

Few countries present a more beautiful variety of scenery than New Caledonia. Stuart's Lake and its environs I have already attempted to describe, but many such landscapes present themselves in different parts of the country, where towering mountains, hill and dale, forest and lake, and verdant plains, blended together in the happiest manner, are taken in by the eye at a glance. Some scenes there are that recall forcibly to the remembrance of a son of Scotia, the hills and glens and "bonnie braes" of his own poor, yet beloved native land. New Caledonia, however, has the advantage over the Old, of being generally well wooded, and possessed of lakes of far greater magnitude; unfortunately, however, the woods are decaying rapidly, particularly several varieties of fir, which are being destroyed by an insect that preys on the bark: when the country is denuded of this ornament, and its ridges have become bald, it will present a very desolate appearance. In some parts of the country, the poplar and aspen tree are to be found, together with a species of birch, of whose bark canoes are built; but there is neither hard wood nor cedar.

Such parts of the district as are not in the immediate vicinity of the regions of eternal snow, yield a variety of wild fruit, grateful to the palate, wholesome, and nutritious. Of these, the Indian pear is the most abundant, and most sought after, both by natives and whites; when fully ripe, it is of a black colour, with somewhat of a reddish tinge, pear-shaped, and very sweet to the taste. The natives dry them in the sun, and afterwards bake them into cakes, which are said to be delicious; for my own part, having seen the process of manufacturing them, I could not overcome my prejudices so far as to partake of a delicacy in whose composition filth formed so considerable an ingredient. When dried, the cakes are placed in wooden vessels to receive the juice of green fruit, which is expressed by placing weights upon it, in wooden troughs, from which spouts of bark draw off the liquid into the vessels containing the dry fruit; this being thoroughly saturated, is again bruised with the unclean hand, then re-formed into cakes, and dried again; and these processes are repeated alternately, until the cakes suit the taste of the maker. Blue berries are plentiful in some parts of the district; there is a peculiar variety of them, which I preferred to any fruit I ever tasted; it is about the size of a musket-ball, of a purple colour, translucid, and in its taste sweet and acid are deliciously blended.

The district is still rich in fur-bearing animals, especially beavers and martens, which are likely to continue numerous for many years to come, as they find a safe retreat among the fastnesses of the Rocky Mountains, where they multiply undisturbed. This is the great beaver nursery, which continues to replace the numbers destroyed in the more exposed situations; there is, nevertheless, a sensible decrease in the returns of the fur since the introduction of steel traps among the natives: there are also otters, musk-rats, minxes, and lynxes. Of the larger quadrupeds bears only are numerous, and in all their varieties, grizzled, black, brown, and chocolate: numbers of them are taken by the natives in wooden traps. A chance moose or reindeer is sometimes found. The mountain sheep generally keeps aloft in the most inaccessible parts of the mountains, and is seldom "bagged" by a Carrier, but often by the Tsekanies. I have before observed that rabbits sometimes abound. Another small animal, whose flesh is delicious in season, the marmot, is found in great numbers. In the neighbourhood of Fort Alexandria, the jumping deer, or chevreuil, is abundant. To these add dog and horse flesh, and you have all the varieties of animal food the country affords to its inhabitants, civilized or savage.

A most destructive little animal, the wood-rat, infests the country, and generally nestles in the crevices of the rocks, but prefers still more human habitations; they domicile under the floors of out-buildings, and not content with this, force their way into the inside, where they destroy and carry off every thing they can; nor is there any way of securing the property in the stores from their depredations but by placing it in strong boxes. When fairly located, it is almost impossible to root them out. They are of a grey colour, and of nearly the size and form of the common rat, but the tail resembles that of the ground squirrel.

The birds of this country are the same as in Canada. I observed no strange variety, except a species of curlieu that frequents the plains of Fort Alexandria in the summer. Immense flocks of cranes are seen in autumn and spring, flying high in the air; in autumn directing their flight towards the south, and in spring towards the north.

Some of the Lakes abound in fish; the principal varieties are trout, carp, white fish, and pike. Stuart's Lake yields a small fish termed by the Canadians "poisson inconnu;" it seems as if it were partly white fish and partly carp, the head resembling the former; it is full of small bones, and the flesh soft and unsavoury. The sturgeon has been already mentioned, but they are unfortunately too rare; seldom more than five or six are captured in a season; they weigh from one hundred to five hundred pounds. A beautiful small fish of the size of the anchovy, and shaped like a salmon, is found in a river that falls into Stuart's Lake; it is said they pass the winter in the lake, and ascend their favourite stream in the month of June, where they deposit their spawn. They have the silvery scales of the larger salmon, and are exceedingly rich; but the natives preserve them almost exclusively for their own use. There are four varieties of salmon, distinguished from each other by the peculiar form of the head; the largest species seems to be the same we have in the rivers of Britain, and weighs from ten to twenty pounds; the others do not exceed half that weight.

New Caledonia is inhabited by the Takelly or Carrier nation, and by a few families of Tsekanies on the north-eastern extremity of the district. The Takellies are divided into as many tribes as there are posts—viz. eight, who formerly were as hostile to each other as if they had been of different nations. The presence of the whites, however, has had the beneficial effect of checking their cut-throat propensities, although individual murders still occasionally occur among them.

Before the introduction of fire-arms, the *honourable* practice of duelling prevailed among them, though in a fashion peculiar to themselves. One arrow only was discharged, by the party demanding satisfaction, at his opponent, who, by dint of skipping about and dodging from side to side, generally contrived to escape it; fatal duels, therefore, seldom if ever occurred; and the parties, having thus given and received satisfaction, retired from the field reconciled.19 They appear more prone to sudden bursts of passion than most Indians I have seen, and quarrel often and abuse each other in the most scurrilous terms. With the Sauteux, Crees, and other tribes on the east side of the mountains, few words are uttered before the blow, often a fatal one, is given; whereas, with the Takellies, it is often many words and few blows. In the quarrels which take place among them, the ladies are generally the *causa belli*—a cause which would soon lead to the depopulation of the country, were all husbands to avenge their wrongs by shedding the blood of the guilty.

Their chiefs have still considerable authority; but much of the homage they claimed and received in former times is now transferred to the white chiefs, or traders, whom they all esteem the greatest men in the universe. "After the Man of heaven," said old Guaw to Mr. Dease, "you are next in dignity." Owing to the superstitious notions of the people, the chiefs are still feared on account of the magical powers ascribed to them; it is firmly believed they can, at will, inflict diseases, cause misfortunes of every kind, and even death itself; and so strong is this impression, that they will not even pass in a direction where the shadow of a chief, or "man of medicine," might fall on them, "lest," say they, "he should bear us some ill-will and afflict us with some disease."

These conjurors, nevertheless, are the greatest bunglers at their trade of any in the Indian territory; they practise none of the clever tricks of the Sauteux sorcerers, and are perfectly ignorant of the medicinal virtues of herbs and plants, with which the Sauteux and other Indians often perform astonishing cures. The Takellies administer no medicine to the sick; a variety of ridiculous gesticulations, together with singing, blowing, and *beating* on the *patient*, are the means they adopt to effect their end; and they, not seldom, effectually cure the patient of "all the ills of life." Whether they effect a cure or not, they are sure to be well recompensed for their expenditure of wind, an article of which they are not sparing: they, in fact, exert themselves so much that the perspiration pours from every pore. The only real remedy they use, in common with other Indians, is the vapour-bath, or sweating-house. The house, as it is termed, which is constructed by bending twigs of willow, and fixing both ends in the ground, when finished, presents the appearance of a bee-hive, and is carefully covered to prevent the escape of the vapour; red-hot stones are then placed inside, and water poured upon them, and the patient remains in the midst of the steam thus generated as long as he can bear it, then rushing out, plunges into the cold stream. This is said to be a sovereign remedy for rheumatism, and the natives have recourse to it in all cases of severe pain: I myself witnessed its efficacy in a case of paralysis.

The salubrity of the climate, however, renders disease of every kind extremely rare, except such as are caused by the excesses of the natives themselves. The venereal is very common, and appears to have been indigenous. At their feasts they gorge themselves to such a degree as to endanger their lives; after a feast many of the guests continue ill for a considerable time, yet this does not prevent them from gormandizing again whenever an opportunity presents itself. Old and young, male and female, are subject to severe inflammation in the eyes, chiefly, I believe, from their passing the winter in hovels underground, which have no outlet for the smoke, and passing from them into the glare of sunshine upon the snow. What with the confined smoke and tainted atmosphere of these abominable burrows, I found it painful to remain even for a few minutes in them.

It has been remarked by those who first settled in the district, that the Indians are rapidly decreasing in numbers since their arrival—a fact which does not admit of a doubt: I myself have seen many villages and encampments without an inhabitant. But what can be the cause of it? Here there has been neither rum nor small-pox—the scourges of this doomed race in other parts. Yet, on the banks of the Columbia, which, when first visited by the whites a few years ago. literally swarmed with Indians, a disease broke out which nearly exterminated them. Has the fiat, then, gone forth, that the aboriginal inhabitants of America shall make way for another race of men? To my mind, at least, the question presents not the shadow of a doubt. The existence of the present race of Indians at some future, and by no means distant period, will only be known through the historical records of their successors.

The Takellies do not use canoes on their hunting excursions, so that they are necessitated to carry all their conveniences on their backs; and it is astonishing to see what heavy loads they can carry, especially the women, on whom the transport duty generally devolves. Among this tribe, however, the women are held in much higher consideration than among other Indians: they assist at the councils, and some ladies of distinction are even admitted to the feasts. This consideration they doubtless owe to the efficient aid they afford in procuring the means of subsistence. The one sex is as actively employed during the fishing season as the other. The men construct the weirs, repair them when necessary, and capture the fish; the women split them up—a most laborious operation when salmon is plentiful—suspend them on the scaffolds, attend to the drying, &c. They also collect berries, and dig up the edible roots that are found in the country, and which are of great service in years of scarcity. Thus the labour of the women contributes as much to the support of the community as that of the men.

The men are passionately addicted to gambling, staking everything they possess, and continuing at it night and day, until compelled to desist by sheer hunger, or by the loss of all. I could not understand their game; we, in fact, used our best endeavours to abolish the pernicious custom, and, to avoid countenancing it, were as seldom present as possible. It is played with a few small sticks, neatly carved, with a certain number of marks upon them, tied up in a small bundle of hay, which the player draws out successively, throws up and catches between his hands; and when all are drawn, they are taken up one by one, and dashed against a piece of parchment, and rolled up again in the hay.

The whole party appear merry enough at the commencement of the game, all joining chorus in a song, and straining their lungs to such a degree, that hoarseness soon ensues, when they continue their amusement in silence. When the game is ended, some of them present a sad spectacle; coming forth, their hair dishevelled, their eyes bloodshot, and faces ghastly pale, with probably nothing to cover their nakedness, save perhaps an old siffleux robe, which the winner may be generous enough to bestow. They never shoot or hang themselves, let their luck be ever so bad, but sometimes shoot the winning party.

Dogs, if not held sacred, are at least as much esteemed by them as their own kindred. I have known an instance of a quadruped of the cynic sect being appointed successor to a biped chief, and discharging the duties of his office with the utmost gravity and decorum; appearing at the feast given in honour of his deceased predecessor, and furnishing his quota—(this of course by proxy)—of the provisions. This dog-chief was treated by his owner with as much regard as if he had been his child! All, indeed, treat their dogs with the greatest respect, calling them by the most endearing epithets:—"Embark, my son;" "Be quiet, my child;" "Don't bark at the white men, they will not harm you."

The lewdness of the Carrier women cannot possibly be carried to a greater excess. They are addicted to the most abominable practices; abandoning themselves in early youth to the free indulgence of their passions, they soon become debilitated and infirm; and there can be no doubt that to this monstrous depravity the depopulation of the country may, in part, be ascribed.

They never marry until satiated with indulgence; and if the woman then should be dissatisfied with the restraint of the conjugal yoke, the union, by mutual consent, is dissolved for a time; both then betake themselves to their former courses. The woman, nevertheless, dare not, according to law, take another husband during this temporary separation. Whoever infringes this law, forfeits his life to the aggrieved party, if he choose, or dare to take it.

Polygamy is allowed; but only one of the women is considered as the wife. The most perfect harmony seems to subsist among them. When the favourite happens to be supplanted by a rival, she resigns her place without a murmur, well pleased if she can only enjoy the countenance of her lord in a subordinate situation. Yet a rupture does sometimes occur, when the repudiated party not unfrequently destroys herself. Suicides were frequent among the females in the neighbourhood of Fort Alexandria.

The Takellies are a sedentary people, remaining shut up in their huts during the severer part of the winter. You may then approach a camp without perceiving any sign of its vicinity, until you come upon their well, or one of their salmon *caches*. They are very social, congregating at each other's huts, and passing their time talking or sleeping. When awake, their tongues are ever in motion,—all bawling out at the same time; and it has often surprised me how they could possibly make themselves understood in the midst of such an uproar.

All Indians with whom I have come in contact, Christian as well as Pagan, are addicted to falsehood; but the Takellies excel; they are perfect adepts in the art, telling their stories with such an appearance of truth, that even those who know them well are often deceived. They were the greatest thieves in the world when the whites first settled among them. The utmost vigilance failed to detect them. Some of our people have been known to have their belts taken off them, without perceiving it till too late; and many a poor fellow, after passing a night in one of their encampments, has been obliged to pass the remainder of the winter with but half a blanket—the other half having been cut off while he slept.

Theft, however, is not quite so prevalent as formerly; and, strange to say, no Indians can be more honest in paying their debts. It would indeed be desirable that this credit system, long since introduced, were abolished; but if this were done, the natives would carry the greater part of their hunts to another quarter. Some of the natives of the coast, having become regular traders of late years, penetrate a considerable distance into the interior; in this manner the goods obtained from the Company's posts along the coast, or from foreign trading ships, pass from hand to hand in barter, until they eventually reach the borders of New Caledonia, where the trade still affords a very handsome profit to the native speculator.

These Indians are not given to hospitality in the proper sense of the word. A stranger arriving among them is provided with food for a day only; should he remain longer, he pays for it; for that day's entertainment, however, the best fare is liberally furnished. Strangers invited to their feasts are also provided for while they remain.

There is much more variety and melody in the airs they sing, than I have heard in any other part of the Indian country. They have professed composers, who turn their talent to good account on the occasion of a feast, when new airs are in great request, and are purchased at a high rate. They dance in circles, men and women promiscuously, holding each other by the hand; and keeping both feet together, hop a little to a side all at once, giving at the same time a singular jerk to their persons behind. The movement seems to be difficult of execution, as it causes them to perspire profusely; they, however, keep excellent time, and the blending of the voices of the men and women in symphony has an agreeable effect.

The Takelly, or Carrier language is a dialect of the Chippewayan; and it is rather a singular fact, that the two intervening dialects of the Beaver Indians and Tsekanies, kindred nations, should differ more from the Chippewayan than the Carrier; the two latter nations being perfectly intelligible to each other, while the former are but very imperfectly understood by their immediate neighbours, the Chippewayans.

An erroneous opinion seems to have gone abroad regarding the variety of languages spoken by the Indians. There are, in reality, only four radically distinct languages from the shores of Labrador to the Pacific: Sauteux, Chippewayan, Atna and Chinook. The Cree language is evidently a dialect of the Sauteux, similar in construction, and differing only in the modification of a few words. The Nascopies, or mountaineers of Labrador, speak a mixture of Cree and Sauteux, the former predominating.

Along the communication from Montreal to the foot of the Rocky Mountains, following the Peace River route, we first meet with the Sauteux tribes, who extend from the Lake of the Two Mountains to Lake Winnipeg; then the Crees to Isle à la Crosse; after them, Crees and Chippewayans to Athabasca; and along the banks of Peace River, the Beaver Indians occupy the lower, and the Tsekanies the upper part. The Chippewayan is evidently the root of the Beaver, Tsekany and Carrier dialects; it is also spoken by a numerous tribe in the McKenzie's River district—the Hare Indians.

On the west side of the Rocky Mountains the Carrier language is succeeded by the Atna, which extends along the Columbia as far down, as the Chinooks, who inhabit the coast. The Atna language, in its variety of dialects, seems to have as wide a scope as either the Sauteux or Chippewayan.

New Caledonia is one of the richest districts in the Company's vast domain; its returns average about 8,000 beavers, with a fair proportion of other valuable furs. When the district was first settled, the goods required for trade were brought in by the winterers from Lac la Pluie, which was their dépôt. The people left the district as early in spring as the navigation permitted, and returned so late that they were frequently overtaken by winter ere they reached their destination. Cold, hunger, and fatigue, were the unavoidable consequences; but the enterprising spirit of the men of those days—the intrepid, indefatigable adventurers of the North-West Company—overcame every difficulty. It was that spirit that opened a communication across the broad continent of America; that penetrated to the frostbound regions of the Arctic circle; and that established a trade with the natives in this remote land, when the merchandise required for it was in one season transported from Montreal to within a short distance of the Pacific. Such enterprise has never been exceeded, seldom or never equalled. The outfit is now sent out from England by Cape Horn, to Fort Vancouver, thence it is conveyed in boats to Okanagan, then transported on horses' backs to Alexandria, the lower post of the district, whence it is conveyed in boats to Fort St. James.

There are generally two commissioned gentlemen in this district,—a chief-factor and chief-trader, with six or seven clerks in charge of posts; and about forty men, principally Iroquois and half-breeds. The fare at the different posts depends entirely on local circumstances. In some places it is tolerable, in others, scarcely fit for dogs. For the year's consumption, the Company allow a clerk two bags of flour, sixty pounds of sugar, twelve pounds of tea, and a small quantity of wine and brandy. Butter is now produced in abundance in the district. Where there are no gardens, the men have only dried salmon,—as poor fare as civilized man subsists on in any part of the world. It has at first the same effect on most people as if they fed on Glauber salts. Nevertheless, the men generally continue in this wretched condition for many years, apparently contented and happy; the indulgence they find among the females being, I grieve to say, the principal inducement.

> **Footnote 19:** I would recommend this mode of conducting "affairs of honour" to *honourable* gentlemen using the hair-trigger, as an improvement. Though practised by savages, it must be allowed to be somewhat less barbarous than ten paces' distance, and standing still! If the exhibition should appear somewhat ludicrous, both parties would have the additional "satisfaction" that their morning *exercise* had given a keener zest to their breakfast. It would be a sort of Pyrrhic dance.